MANAGING PROJECTS

Managing Projects

CHRIS and JANE CHURCHOUSE

A Gower Management Workbook

Published by
Gower Publishing Limited
Gower House
Croft Road
Aldershot
Hampshire GU1 3HR
England

Gower
Old Post Road
Brookfield
Vermont 05036
USA

British Library Cataloguing in Publication Data

Churchouse, Chris
    Managing projects. – (A Gower management workbook)
    1. Industrial project management
    I. Title II. Churchouse, Jane
    658.4'04

ISBN 0 566 08098 2

Typeset by MindShift Ltd and printed in Great Britain by
MPG Books Limited, Bodmin, Cornwall.

Contents

PART I — 'I've just been told I'm a project manager!' What to do at the start of your project to maximize your chances of success

PART II — 'Projects are about people' Making your project happen

PART III

'Is this goodbye – or just au revoir?'
What to do to finish your project and
how to evaluate its success

Preface

During the past few years, the label 'project manager' has been stuck onto more people than ever before. Many have no idea of what a project manager is – or the difference between managing a project and managing anything else. In too many cases, the title has been given to show that the organization is 'with-it', using the latest buzz words – but without substance to back it up.

To help you decide whether you are working on a project, take a look at these questions.

- ❖ Is the work you are performing constrained to finish by a specified date?
- ❖ Does it produce something or change something?
- ❖ Does it use resources (people, money, equipment, materials)?
- ❖ Is it important – to you or someone else?
- ❖ Has someone referred to it as a project?

If you have answered 'Yes' to two or more of these questions, this Workbook is for you.

We have taken the approach that, in most cases, the first indication that you are a project manager will be when your own manager tells you that you are to manage a project! The Workbook therefore gives you some guidance on what to do at the start, to clarify your own position, and then takes you through the whole lifecycle of a project.

We have used techniques from a wide range of sources, gained over many years' experience. In particular, we have drawn upon the PRINCE 2 method in some places and have developed or expanded from it. PRINCE is a Registered Trade Mark of CCTA and you will find a reference on the final page of the Workbook.

The Workbook is divided into Parts, to coincide with the three major stages of a project, and Units, to cover each of the principal tasks or issues in managing that stage. The Fast Track sections give you some practical, quickly-assimilated advice on what to do when you are under pressure. The Skillbuilder sections offer longer-term guidance on how to make sure that future tasks are properly planned and executed. Finally, the Check Points at the end of each Part are there to help you solve some of the most common problems.

Thank you for choosing to read *Managing Projects*. We hope you enjoy it. Good luck!

Chris and Jane Churchouse

Acknowledgements

Our thanks are due to the many organizations that have erred in their approach to project management and have repeated their errors so consistently. They provide headlines for our national newspapers and our research would be the poorer without them.

Our thanks are also due to our clients, who have provided opportunities for our experiments and who have proved to us that projects *can* be managed successfully.

About the Authors

Chris Churchouse

Chris holds a Degree in Mathematics and Technology and a Master's Degree in Business Administration (MBA). He is a member of the British Computer Society and the Institute of Management - for which he has been local Branch Chairman. He has been active in both organizations at national level, in various committees and working parties. He is currently a member of the PRINCE Examination Board, on which he represents the PRINCE User Group.

His working career has encompassed spells in both the private and public sectors with organizations such as Dexion, Westland Helicopters and the Ministry of Defence, concentrating initially on engineering and information technology and, latterly, on the people side of project management. He is a qualified PRINCE project management practitioner and a Chartered IS Engineer. Chris is also a Director of Mind*Shift* Ltd, having laid the foundation for the organization in October 1986.

Jane Churchouse

Jane holds an Honours Degree, a Master's Degree in Business Administration (MBA), various teaching and training qualifications, NVQs in Management and in Training and certificates in psychometric testing. She is a Fellow of the Institute of Personnel and Development - for which she sits on the National Membership and Education Committee - and has been an External Verifier for an NVQ Awarding Body.

Jane's background is in personnel, training and line management with organizations such as British Airports Authority, Racal Telecom and the Department of Employment. She is now a Director of Mind*Shift* Ltd. where she specializes in providing consultancy and training in management and the implementation and delivery of NVQs.

'I've just been told I'm a project manager!'

What to do at the start of your project to maximize your chances of success

By the end of this Part you will be able to:

- define the scope of your project – what is included and what is not

- recognize the various stakeholders and how they have an influence on your project

- determine what authority you require to proceed and what approval mechanisms exist

- define your project's deliverables

- determine the timescales and resources you need

- understand the risks to your project and how to deal with them.

If you are confident that you can already answer 'Yes' to most or all of the following questions you might like simply to refresh your memory by scanning the Fast Track pages in each Unit and then move on to Part II.

Self assessment checklist: Part I	
I am confident that I can:	**Yes ☑ No ☒**
Define the scope and objectives of my project.	
Name the main stakeholders in my project and state what their interest is.	
State my own level of responsibility and authority and who I need to refer to outside of these limits.	
Describe how to define project deliverables in such a way as to aid planning, progress control and quality control.	
Work out how to schedule the project, allocate resources efficiently and estimate timescales and costs accurately.	
Identify the main risks to this project and define management and contingent actions to deal with them.	

UNIT 1 What to do Prior to Planning

In this Unit, we will be covering the actions you need to take when you have been allocated a potential project.

- **Determine its justification and scope.**
- **Identify the main stakeholders and define their influence on the project.**
- **Clarify the levels of authority in the project.**
- **Identify your priorities.**

Understanding these actions will help you:

- decide whether or not you have a viable project
- enlist the support of appropriate people
- decide what actions you can take and what you must refer to others
- make decisions that are appropriate to the project
- avoid problems with unauthorized expenditure or activity.

What to do prior to planning

STEP 1: DETERMINE YOUR PROJECT'S JUSTIFICATION AND SCOPE

Projects do not normally emerge from thin air – someone will have identified a need or opportunity which you, as project manager, will be expected to fulfil. Therefore, as manager of a new project your very first job will be to find out the overall justification for your project.

This justification could be expressed in financial or some other terms.

For example:

This project will implement a revised customer service charter that will result in lower administration costs and higher customer satisfaction.

In this case, you will need to define what savings in administration costs you are looking for and you may also be able to define measures for customer satisfaction. These are the benefits that your project is expected to bring to the organization.

Find out what your own project's justification is and write the details in the boxes provided.

Statement of justification		
Benefits sought		
Financial savings	Other financial	Non-financial

Now that you know the reasoning behind your project you will need to define its scope – what is included and what is not.

Your next questions will therefore be:

1	**2**	**3**
What will this project encompass?	What will not form part of this project?	What other limitations will you have to work within?

For example:

The customer service charter project will encompass the production of a revized customer service charter with associated operating procedures for customer service personnel.

It will extend to customer service personnel only and will not encompass staff in other departments. It will not extend to third parties who perform servicing on contract to us.

The project will need to complete its objectives within nine months from the start date to meet expected new consumer legislation requirements.

Once you have established these you can write them in the table on the next page. Add the constraints under which you will be working, together with a note of where these constraints came from so that, if things change, you will be able to identify any knock-on effects on the project.

What's in?	What's out?
What's a constraint?	**Where did the constraint come from?**

STEP 2: IDENTIFY YOUR PROJECT'S STAKEHOLDERS

A stakeholder is anyone who has an influence over your project or who is influenced by it. Your task now is to construct your own stakeholder table. Your table should include people who will take different roles in your project.

Using the table on the following page, write in the left column the name of each stakeholder you identify.

In the next column, make a note of what they bring to the project – which could be finance, authority, political support, staff, equipment, knowledge or similar. Be as specific as you can.

In the next column, list what they receive from the project. This might be a deliverable, but could be a new way of working or a reduction in staff, for instance. It might be that they will lose their job – or gain a promotion.

The next column is for you to state whether they are likely to be in favour of the project, against it or neutral.

Finally, the right column gives you space to record how you will deal with this person. Will you gain their commitment, report to them, supply project news on a regular basis, negotiate with them, direct or force them – or simply ignore them?

Keep your table confidential. For this reason it is better to take a photocopy and write on that, rather than write in this Workbook.

Stakeholder Table

Person	What do they bring to the project?	What do they get from the project?	Are they likely to be supportive, neutral or hostile?	How will you involve them?

STEP 3: CLARIFY LEVELS OF AUTHORITY

Very often you may have the authority to make a decision within certain bounds in terms of time, cost and quality, and some level of authority over your staff. You now need to determine:

What are the limits to your authority in this project?

What should you do when decisions are needed outside these limits?

Your organization may have guidelines on this already, or you may need to get clarification from elsewhere.

**Action Point**

Take the time now to investigate your organization's authorization procedures. You may like to incorporate them into a project manual or guidelines.

Now complete the checklist on the following page. If you can make your own decisions, simply tick the second column. If you have an authority limit, say what that limit is in the third column. If you must refer the matter to someone else write that person's name in the final column.

There is space at the end of the checklist for you to add further items if necessary.

Check List of Responsibilities

When it comes to	✓ I decide	I decide within stated bounds	I refer to stated person
Selecting project staff			
Directing project staff			
Approving staff leave			
Approving staff overtime			
Approving staff expenses			
Accepting changes to the project's scope or deliverables			
Approving delays to completion			
Approving overspends			
Signing contracts with suppliers			
Agreeing contractual changes with suppliers			
Approving specifications of deliverables			
Closing the project			

STEP 4: IDENTIFY YOUR PRIORITIES

Projects are usually required to deliver something to a set level of quality within a predetermined time and with a limited amount of money. However, when things do not work out, at least one of these must give. Which will it be?

For example, Lucy's project is to organize a conference on a specific date which she is not able to alter. If the project is not running to plan she will therefore have to spend more or reduce quality.

For your own project, ask the questions:

a

What are the relative priorities of any constraints?

b

If something has to 'give' what will this be?

 Action Point

Place a cross in the triangle. The closer the cross to a constraint, the more it can be moved. (The example shown demonstrates a view that time is unchangeable and that cost and quality can be moved – cost more than quality.)

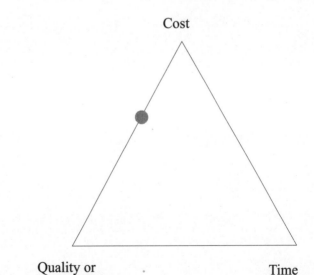

Cost

Quality or functionality

Time

YOU MAY NOW CONTINUE WITH THE NEXT UNIT ON PAGE 23 OR MOVE TO THE SKILLBUILDER SECTION THAT FOLLOWS

FAST TRACK

What to do prior to planning

STEP 1: DETERMINE YOUR PROJECT'S JUSTIFICATION AND SCOPE

We started off this Unit by recommending that you make sure that you know your project's justification and scope.

Some of the reasons for doing this are:

1

You will have a better chance of succeeding if you know what you are aiming at

2

You will be better able to avoid doing unnecessary (or unwanted) work

3

If your project fits in with other projects or other work within the organization, you need to ensure that there is no overlap and no gaps

Most of the work in this step involves collecting information. For example, you will need to know on what basis to calculate the financial benefits. You will need to find out what other projects are running, and what are being planned. How will you go about collecting this information, and from where?

Your starting point is to ask the person or group who assigned the project to you. They might well have additional information that you would find useful such as a feasibility study report, a consultancy report, corporate (or departmental) objectives, a programme management plan or such like. They may also have a very clear idea of the benefits they are seeking.

 Star Tip

Any project must meet three criteria: will it work, does it make business sense and is it what we want?

You will find other sources of information both within the organization and from outside it.

Internal

- ❖ Company reports, for:
  - • Financial information, such as the cost of borrowing, overheads as a proportion of staff costs, the cost of some capital items, numbers of staff, average salaries, heating and other consumable costs. You may need to do some calculations and make some assumptions, however.
  - • Plans for the future, which might give an indication of likely priorities for this project, or related projects.
  - • Constraints especially legal, social and environmental.
- ❖ Departmental objectives, for:
  - • Measurable objectives in terms of outcomes.
  - • Cost and resource constraints.
- ❖ Consultancy reports.
- ❖ Organigrams (to show the organizational structure).
- ❖ Other published information such as staff cost ready reckoners, transfer costs and standard discount factors.

External

- ❖ Estimates and quotations from suppliers.
- ❖ Company reports for other organizations, showing how they have done something similar or what benefits they are claiming.
- ❖ Industry reports, showing trends and also the levels of benefit other organizations have found from certain types of work.
- ❖ Advertisements and news reports, for background knowledge.
- ❖ Professional institutes, for best practice advice and sometimes for unbiased information about what works and what doesn't.
- ❖ Supplier literature, for details of equipment, consumables and costs.
- ❖ The Internet, for vast amounts of the above information.
- ❖ Local public libraries.

The first time I was asked to prepare a project plan, I didn't know how to produce a cost/benefit analysis. I went to the library closest to where I worked and read some books on it. Then I returned to the office and dug out some costs from suppliers, plus their claims of what our savings would be. I was able to justify the project and, as a bonus, noticed an error in the supplier's calculations which, when corrected, resulted in a cost reduction for the equipment.

Once you have established the justification and scope of your project you are in a better position to decide just what your project needs to produce. We will be looking at this in the next Unit.

Finally, you will remember that we suggested making a note of where any constraints on your project have come from. Without an understanding of where a constraint came from, the project is likely to keep on going when the requirement for it has disappeared, or decisions will be made on the basis of a need that no longer exists. If your constraint is financial, you should still state why that particular amount of money has been chosen.

Activity

Consider the Customer Service example from the Fast Track.

What constraint is dependent on the external environment?

What could happen to reduce or eliminate the need for this project?

SKILLBUILDER

The project is gearing up for legislative changes which may not happen – say, if the government were to fall or the European Union were to get involved – or may get pushed back into a later parliamentary session. If the project manager is conscious of this constraint they can keep an eye on the legislative climate and adjust their responses accordingly.

Having an understanding of where a constraint came from will also give you some indication of how likely it is that it can be lifted. For example, many projects are given a constraint of a particular end date. However, if the logic is strong enough it may well be possible for you to agree an extension.

STEP 2: IDENTIFY YOUR PROJECT'S STAKEHOLDERS

We have said that stakeholders are people with some sort of vested interest in your project. Without the support of your key stakeholders you will struggle to make the project succeed. With a powerful stakeholder against you, some form of failure is almost inevitable.

It is therefore important for any project organization to have a clear understanding of who their stakeholders are because they are likely to be in a position to influence its direction and success.

There may be many types of stakeholder, both from within and outside your organization.

 **Activity**

Decide whether each of the following represents an internal or external stakeholder. Underline the internal stakeholders.

managers   suppliers

staff

partners   beneficiaries

users   rivals

onlookers

losers   gatekeepers

customers

interest groups   collaborators

Internal stakeholders

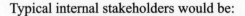

Typical internal stakeholders would be:

❖ Staff who will be working on the project perhaps full-time or maybe only part of the time
❖ Managers with a role in directing the project and supplying resources to it
❖ Beneficiaries or users
❖ Onlookers – those interested in it but not affected by it.
❖ Those who stand to lose from the project
❖ Gatekeepers to any of these people

External stakeholders

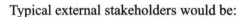

Typical external stakeholders would be:

❖ Customers and suppliers of products, services, information or knowledge that the project requires
❖ Special interest groups such as environmentalists
❖ Rival organizations
❖ Potential collaborators

One way of identifying potential stakeholders is to ask three questions:

1

Who has an interest in making sure that this project achieves its goals?

2

Who has an interest in making sure that it does not achieve its goals?

3

Who has an interest in skewing those goals to their own advantage?

We have already noted that the various stakeholders may well have differing interests in your project:

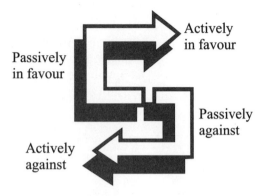

Passively
in favour

Actively
in favour

Actively
against

Passively
against

Active+

You need to ensure that these people stay that way. However, you also need to be aware that they might try to keep the project going even when the need for it has disappeared.

Passive+

You may need to persuade these people to 'cast their vote' if needed. They can be powerful allies but you will need to tell them why their support is needed and what to do about it.

Active-

You will need to tackle these people according to their objections. Sometimes you can do this by logical argument but more often you will need to change their attitudes about the project (which is difficult) or simply outweigh their influence. This is where you can call upon the passively in favour to 'outvote' them.

Passive-

These people may be a deadening influence, proving difficult or impossible to get things through. They are likely to do nothing about responding to your requests to help or providing acceptance for project deliverables. You may need to stand over them while they provide what you need from them.

STEP 3: CLARIFY LEVELS OF AUTHORITY

This is a very important activity. By clarifying your own level of authority you will ensure that you neither exceed it nor waste time referring decisions upwards. Also, by knowing what levels of authority exist above you, you will be able to determine the likely consequences of any proposals for change.

For example, if you are considering an extra expenditure of £3 000 and this is within your authority, you can base your decision on the costs and benefits. If you need to refer this upwards to your manager, you may also have to consider the time this will take. If you know that your manager will have to refer the decision upwards to a project strategy committee or board and they might make fundamental changes to the project scope and objectives, this might affect your decision even to propose the expenditure in the first place.

If you're unsure of any answers, clarify them with your manager or the project board or by referring to your job description or organizational procedures manual, as appropriate.

Your manager may not be willing (or permitted) to delegate financial powers to you. However, it may be possible to allow you to take some decisions. You should already have an idea about your own level of authority in the organization and it is likely that this will remain much as it is while working on this project.

It is particularly important to understand your level of authority in relation to your staff. Some project managers can hire and fire. Others have to work with the people they are given and have no control over the matter not even being able to discipline them or control their time off.

 Can you?

❖ Take decisions about scheduling the project?
❖ Take decisions about changes to the project?
❖ Allocate work to people?
❖ Place contracts?
❖ Negotiate with suppliers on quality and
functionality issues?
❖ Accept and reject work?
❖ Stop the project?

SKILLBUILDER

Finally, you may also need to understand the unwritten 'cultural' constraints of the project. If staff in your firm always take Friday afternoons off you are unlikely to be in a position to insist that they work, even if the project is running late. If the organization is very hierarchical, you will need to ensure that you communicate up the line, as shortcutting the system may not be possible.

STEP 4: IDENTIFY YOUR PRIORITIES

We have already looked at priorities in terms of time, cost and quality. You may also find it useful to prioritize the benefits you are seeking to achieve as well.

Look back at the statement of justification you wrote earlier and the benefits your project is seeking. If you could only achieve ONE benefit, which would it be? If the project is not viable with only one benefit, choose the top two (or three, until you have identified the smallest number of benefits you could accept).

If you could achieve that and ONE more benefit, which would that be? Continue until you have prioritized them all.

This information will help you in future decision-making during the project.

UNIT 2   Define Your Project's Outcomes

In this Unit, we will be covering a method to assist you in defining precisely what the project outcomes will be, and hence what your plan will focus on.

- **Define outcomes.**
- **Review and agree outcomes.**

Understanding this method will help you:

- make sure that you do not miss any vital outcomes
- develop a sound basis for planning
- communicate your requirements to your project team.

Define your project's outcomes

STEP 1: SPECIFY THE OUTCOMES

In Unit 1 we established the need for your project and what it is expected to achieve. It is now time for us to define these outcomes more clearly so that you can specify your project's 'deliverables' what it is that your project needs to achieve.

For example:

The customer service charter project will deliver:

❖ *A revized customer service charter*

❖ *New operating procedures for customer service personnel*

❖ *A call centre to manage all customer service enquiries*

❖ *A publicity programme to inform all customers of the changes*

Notice that all of these are 'things to be delivered' and not 'work to be done'. This approach is known as 'product based planning' and is the approach that we will be using as we progress through the workbook.

 Action Point

Now spend some time to find out what your project must deliver and write these in the boxes provided.

1.	
2.	
3.	
4.	
5.	
6.	

While these final deliverables are what your project has been set up to deliver, there will be other things that it has to produce along the way and possibly further outcomes that have not yet been identified.

For example, in a project to deliver a corporate Web site, there may be intermediate outcomes such as a list of things to include in the site, a set of graphics, some wording (approved by Marketing), a contract with a service provider and so forth. It may not have been recognized when the project was defined that the Web site will need to be updated from time to time and that someone needs to be responsible for dealing with e-mail enquiries. So there may be further outcomes in terms of a maintenance schedule, a set of organizational responsibilities and even a service level agreement defining response rates to enquiries.

1

What further outcomes intermediate or final will this project need to produce? Who will receive each outcome?

2

Which outcomes are needed before others?

For example, you cannot produce the Web site without the words and the graphics, but these cannot be produced until you have a clear understanding of what is to be included.

Once you have identified your outcomes you are in a position to identify what goes into them.

3

What inputs do you need for each of the outcomes and where will they come from?

4

How will you know when the outcome has been produced to a satisfactory standard? What criteria should you use to assess the outcome against and how can you do this?

For each outcome, fill in one of these forms. (Leave out any section that is obviously irrelevant for the outcome.)

PRODUCT DESCRIPTION

Purpose:

(Why is this item needed?)

Recipient:

(Who will receive this item when complete?)

Composition:

(What will be included in it? Make a list.)

Format:

(What form will it take?)

Derivation:

(Where will the information it relies on come from? Where will any components of it come from? Who will provide these things?)

Quality Criteria:

(What standards must it comply with? What tolerances are there on measurements? How can you define what is acceptable?)

Quality Check:

(What can be done to check the item against the quality criteria? Who will do this?)

STEP 2: REVIEW AND AGREE THE OUTCOMES

We have already gone through the process of identifying the final and intermediate outcomes of your project. Now it is time to review progress so far and ensure that everything fits together as it should.

1

To begin with, reflect on the Stakeholder Analysis you did in Unit 1. Did it include all of the people you have identified as receiving outcomes. If not, add them to your analysis.

2

Can you clearly link the outcomes you have identified with the benefits you listed in Unit 1?

Have you identified which outcomes lead to which benefits?

3

Are there any outcomes that do not appear to link to benefits? Why is the project producing these?

Are there any benefits that appear not to have any outcomes associated with them? How will those benefits happen?

4

Who has an interest in these outcomes? Should you gain their agreement to your plans? How can you keep them informed?

YOU MAY NOW CONTINUE WITH THE NEXT UNIT ON PAGE 37 OR MOVE TO THE SKILLBUILDER SECTION THAT FOLLOWS

Define Your Project's Outcomes

STEP 1: SPECIFY THE OUTCOMES

 **Star Tip**

According to the British Standard BS6079: "One of the major causes of substandard project management arizes from failures at the planning stage, causing a series of subsequent alterations or clarifications that pushes up expenditure and causes delays .... The more planning done before contractual obligations are established the less risk there is of failing to meet those obligations"

You will remember that we suggested in Fast Track that you define your project's outcomes in terms of 'deliverables' rather than processes. This is because you will have difficulty later in measuring progress and success if you use expressions like 'to revize the customer service charter' or 'to create a new operating procedure'. Only by specifying the outcomes will you be in a position to gauge whether you have achieved the project's objectives.

The traditional way of defining a project is to break the work down into similar types to create a Work Breakdown Structure.

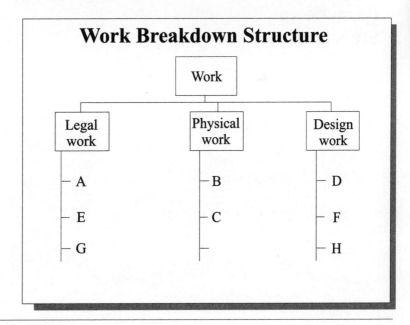

While this is fine in engineering and construction projects it is of little benefit to most office-based projects. Concentrating on what you need to produce is a far more meaningful and useful way of dealing with these – and one that can still be used on the engineering and construction projects as well.

One way of identifying what your project needs to produce is by means of a Product Breakdown Structure (PBS). Using brainstorming or a similar creative technique you identify as many of your project's intermediate and final outcomes as possible and then group them according to type. This makes it easier to identify where products are missing and helps generate ideas about any additional products that might be required.

There are no hard and fast rules about how you group products in a PBS. It doesn't really matter if you use a diagram or some other format – perhaps an indented list. This is a planning aid and you should use it with that intention firmly in your mind. What is important is that:

❖ You show all the products
❖ You group them in a way that
    • helps you understand what is being produced
    • identify any missing products

Here is an example of a PBS for a fruit pie. We will pursue this example further during this Unit.

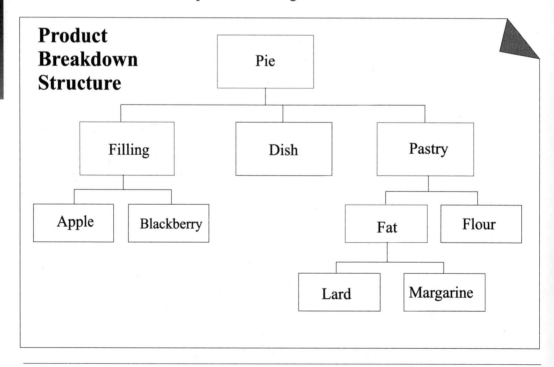

Product Breakdown Structure

As you can see, in this example the pie filling is made up from two ingredients. The pastry is also made up from two ingredients one of which is made up from two ingredients itself. The PBS can therefore show the makeup of a product using groups of products and groups of groups.

If you are a cook, you may also have noticed quite quickly and easily from this PBS that two ingredients are missing from the pastry – water and salt. However, it would be relatively easy to put these in now that you know.

You may have noticed from our pie that, although the PBS shows the products you need in order to produce it, the diagram does not show you how to put these products together. As a total novice in the pastry department, the PBS would not provide me with a great deal of guidance as it stands at the moment. So, having constructed a Product Breakdown Structure, the next task is to produce a Product Flow Diagram (PFD). The Product Flow Diagram shows how all the products rely on each other. At this stage, it does not necessarily indicate the order in which you will produce your products, or where your priorities lie. We will see in a later Unit how you can derive these 'dependencies' for the activities that go into making the products.

Here is our pie again, as a Product Flow Diagram.

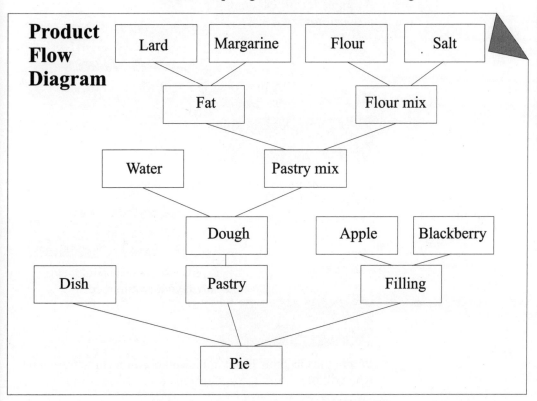

This has proved quite a worthwhile exercise, for now we know that there are some intermediate products in our project: the flour mix, the combined fat, the pastry mix, the dough. It now seems that the filling is also an intermediate product, rather than just a convenient grouping of ingredients. All these intermediate products should now be added to the PBS for completeness.

We are also starting to see the relationships between the various different products which make up the pie. It is, for example, the specification of the combined fat that determines how much margarine to add to how much lard. Note also that the dough is different from the pastry, although no new ingredient has been added. (You doubt me? Try eating it!)

The final part of product based planning consists of writing Product Descriptions (PDs) for each of the products. The PD simply describes each product in words. It is not a detailed specification just a description.

Your product descriptions should include:

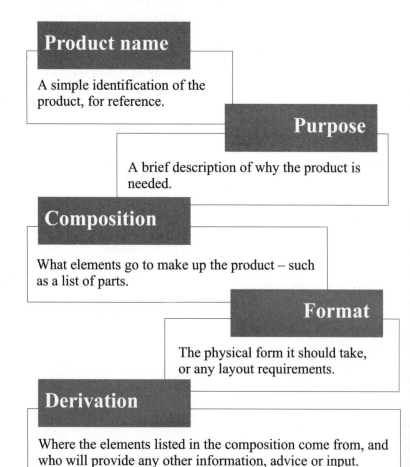

Product name

A simple identification of the product, for reference.

Purpose

A brief description of why the product is needed.

Composition

What elements go to make up the product – such as a list of parts.

Format

The physical form it should take, or any layout requirements.

Derivation

Where the elements listed in the composition come from, and who will provide any other information, advice or input.

Quality criteria

A list of the standards to be complied with – national, organizational, departmental, industrial or ad hoc. Other criteria that can be measured to determine the acceptability of the product. Some typical items to include are:

❖ Does the product contain all of the items listed under composition?
❖ Will it fulfill its purpose?

Quality checks

What checking processes will be performed to ensure that the quality criteria have been met? If quality criteria rely on opinion (such as a product's ease of use) whose opinion will be sought?

People involved

Who is responsible for ensuring this product will be produced?

Who else will be involved in its production?

Who will receive the product when complete?

Who will approve the product?

Who will maintain the product when the project has finished?

We gave a proforma Product Description in Fast Track, and you may like to copy that for your own use.

STEP 2: REVIEW AND AGREE THE OUTCOMES

You will find it easier to gain approval for your project plans if you let people know what you are doing. You may need to gain the approval of your stakeholders, or some of them at least, and providing them with a clear idea of the outcomes is a good way of doing this. Not only does it shorten the time taken to get approval to proceed, it also reduces the likelihood that they will reject the finished article.

Real Life Story

A colleague of ours was asked to undertake a project to develop a selection test for warehouse staff. The client was the Warehouse Manager but the actual budget holder was the Personnel Manager. As the project progressed it emerged that each had a very different view of what was required and, as they were not on speaking terms, our colleague had great difficulty in getting agreement as to what she should do. At one point she had almost determined on producing two sets of outputs – one for the Warehouse Manager and the other for the Personnel Manager! Having talked it through with us, however, she decided to insist on a three-way meeting to resolve the issue and agree a unified specification – and in future she always agreed a precise product description prior to starting any work.

You will also need to communicate the outcomes to those whose job is to work on them in the project. The product description, in particular, is a powerful tool for facilitating this.

Guideline

Choose your communication method to suit the recipient and the type of information. Here are some guidelines to help you decide which to use.

Product description	Conveying detail	Conveying strategy
Meeting	Gaining agreement	Sending bulk information
Memo	General awareness	Introducing sensitive ideas
Charts and diagrams	Simplifying complex ideas	Defining precise details

Star Tip

People will very often respond to communications in the form by which they received them by fax to faxes, by letter to letters. You may like to think through your preferred method of receipt prior to sending out a communication to your stakeholders.

Having reviewed your outcomes, benefits, stakeholder analysis and all other work done to date to make sure that it all fits neatly together you will now be in an excellent position to plan your project.

SKILLBUILDER

UNIT 3 Schedule and Resource Your Project

In this Unit, we will be looking at methods of scheduling work and resources for your project.

- **Estimate what you need for the project.**
- **Sequence the activities.**
- **Assign resources efficiently and effectively.**

Understanding these three factors will help you:

- plan the work in the best sequence, given the resources you have
- assign suitable people to the tasks
- make decisions about workloads later in the project.

Schedule and resource your project

STEP 1: ESTIMATE THE TIME, MONEY AND PEOPLE YOU NEED FOR THE JOB

Now that you have determined what products you need to deliver you are in a position to decide exactly what work these entail. You need to answer three questions.

1 What activities do you need to plan to produce each of the outcomes identified?

2 How long will each activity last?

3 How much will it cost?

If you do not know, how will you find out? Copy the form below and use it to help you collect the information you need.

Action Point

For this product:		
These are the materials and consumables		They cost
These are the processes	They take this long	And cost

Having identified the activities you can now work out the resources that your project will use. These include money, personnel, equipment and consumables. Some of these will be one-offs, such as the purchase of a computer, others periodic – that is, occurring at intervals during the project – such as salaries and annual insurance. You may already have identified some of these in the constraints. However, in this section, they are simply *what you aim to use*.

For example:

The customer service charter project will be staffed by one full-time project manager and three additional staff. Central project support will be available. The project is expected to cost £225 000 excluding the costs of procured equipment and services for the new call centre.

Now complete the table below with the information you have. Make a separate list for each outcome. You may find it useful to write these onto the Product Descriptions – perhaps on the back.

Action Point

Resource needs	One-off costs	Periodic costs
Money: (how much)		
People: (who)		
Equipment: (what)		
Consumables: (what)		
Other: (state)		

STEP 2: SEQUENCE THE ACTIVITIES

Now it is time to decide the order in which you will undertake your activities. This involves checking what must be done in sequence and what can be done in parallel. You therefore need to ask two questions.

What is the logical sequence for performing the work?

Are there any activities that could be performed sooner so as to bring earlier benefits?

You will want to present this information in some meaningful way. One option is to produce a network diagram and find the critical path(s). The Skillbuilder section shows you how to do this.

Other techniques that you could use for scheduling or expressing these plans include Gantt charts or even simply writing the various tasks in the diary.

STEP 3: ASSIGN RESOURCES TO THE WORK REQUIRED

Now you need to decide who will perform each of the activities.

 Check List

Remember to include:

- ❖ Full-time project staff including yourself
- ❖ Part-time project staff with other responsibilities
- ❖ Seconded staff
- ❖ Support staff
- ❖ Contractors
- ❖ Customers who will be taking part in any activity
- ❖ Others such as those who provide resources or approval and whose time delays you will have to cope with.

Star Tip

Computer programs for project scheduling usually allow you to allocate a 'calendar' to each resource, to show when they are available for project work. You may need to take special care if you use this feature, as some programs are not as sensible as you might imagine.

As people differ you will need to look at each one to identify their suitability for the tasks in hand. Here are some factors to consider.

It is often preferable, both from the point of view of the project's costs and for staff morale, to avoid situations which require lots of changes in work patterns. You will therefore want to even out these situations as much as possible so as to produce a work schedule that is acceptable for each resource.

Once you have decided on your resource needs you will need to make sure that each person knows what is expected of them.

How will you do this and how are other stakeholders involved in the plan and kept informed about it?

You may need to add extra activities such as communicating with key customers to your final plans.

Of course, resources are always limited and it may be that you do not receive the number or type that you require. Where this happens you need to make an appropriate response.

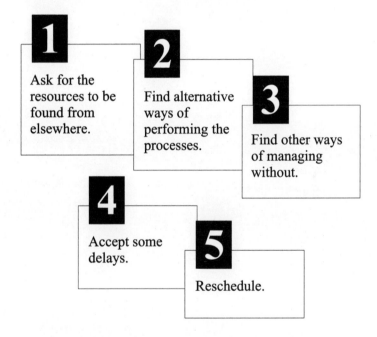

1 Ask for the resources to be found from elsewhere.

2 Find alternative ways of performing the processes.

3 Find other ways of managing without.

4 Accept some delays.

5 Reschedule.

Finally, check your budget.

Will the money be available when you need it? How will you account for this?

Schedule and resource your project

STEP 1: ESTIMATE THE TIME, MONEY AND PEOPLE YOU NEED FOR THE JOB

Now that you know what to do you need to determine what resources you need for each activity. As well as the obvious ones such as time, money and people you might also need to include equipment, consumables, information and work space. You may find that this information has already been provided perhaps in a business case or a report from a feasibility study. If not, you may need to do some calculations for yourself.

Here are some ways of estimating:

1 Use standard timings and costings (if your organization has them).

2 Look at what you or others have done before and make a judgement based on relative size and similarity to your current activity.

3 Ask 'experts' (such as consultants) for their opinion.

4 Perform a small trial and proportion up the results.

5 See how long you've got and divide up your time to suit.

6 See how much money you have and divide it up to suit.

As you will probably have gathered, estimation is necessarily an inexact activity perhaps more of an art than a science. However, there are some guidelines you can use to take some of the guesswork out of it.

 Guideline

Always use at least two methods of estimating.

(Top down takes an overall view whereas bottom up analyses the requirements of each part of an activity in turn and then adds the results together.)

Guideline

Make a start, however unsure you may be.

(You will improve with experience, although your first estimate may be way off. If you don't start because you find it too difficult, it will always remain too difficult.)

Guideline

Don't mistake an estimate for a prediction.

(Estimates are about what could happen. Predictions are about what will happen and we cannot know that.)

Guideline

Keep your estimates pure.

(Don't clutter them with contingencies and allowances. You can add those in later to deal with the vagaries of your organization's approvals systems and other people's propensities to cut your estimates.)

Guideline

Don't confuse precision with accuracy.

(If you start with a guess and multiply it by a factor, you can end up with misleading figures – 11.237 weeks, for instance. The precision misleads people into believing there is more to the estimate than is true. This estimate should really say 11 – 12 weeks.)

Guideline

Include your assumptions.

(If you later want to check the accuracy of an estimate, or modify it to reflect actual performance, you will need this information. So document it.)

STEP 2: SEQUENCE THE ACTIVITIES

Many books on project management focus on the scheduling techniques that exist – network diagrams, Gantt charts and critical path analysis. These were developed in the engineering and construction industries for large, complex projects. They can still be used for smaller projects, but they are significantly less important for these in relation to the other aspects of project management – like dealing with stakeholders, project staff, requests for change, risks and so on.

Nevertheless, you may want to use a simple scheduling technique to help you, and network diagrams can be used in just about any project.

A network diagram is simply a schedule of work, showing what has to be done and when. Although these diagrams are normally produced by computer they can also be done by hand quite simply for many smaller projects. For each step in the process, draw a box (see right) and link it to its predecessors and successors by lines (as in the diagram below). Knowing the elapsed time for each task you can apply a simple two

Earliest start	Duration	Earliest finish
Activity name		
Latest start	Float	Latest finish

stage process first, to obtain the earliest start and finish dates and then, working backwards, to obtain the latest start and finish dates. The difference between earliest and latest dates is known as the float the amount of leeway one has for delay.

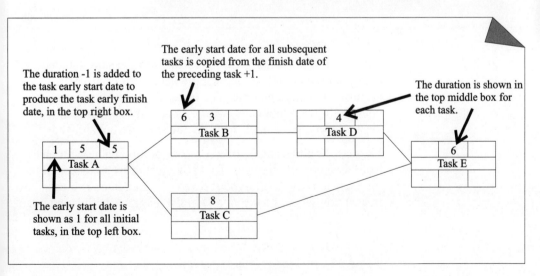

The early start date for all subsequent tasks is copied from the finish date of the preceding task +1.

The duration -1 is added to the task early start date to produce the task early finish date, in the top right box.

The duration is shown in the top middle box for each task.

6	3	
Task B		

	4	
Task D		

1	5	5
Task A		

The early start date is shown as 1 for all initial tasks, in the top left box.

	8	
Task C		

	6	
Task E		

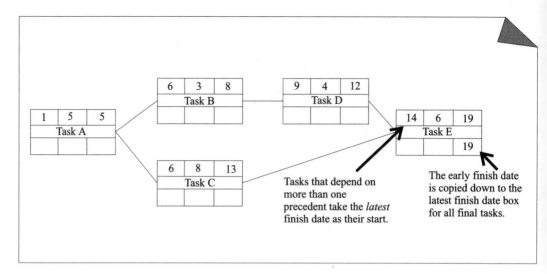

The early finish date is copied down to the latest finish date box for all final tasks.

Tasks that depend on more than one precedent take the *latest* finish date as their start.

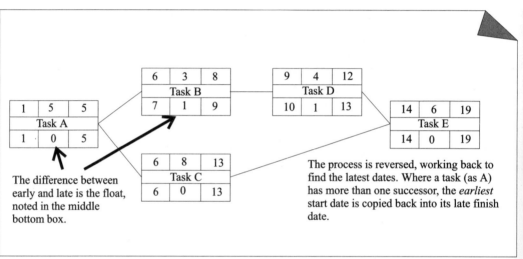

The difference between early and late is the float, noted in the middle bottom box.

The process is reversed, working back to find the latest dates. Where a task (as A) has more than one successor, the *earliest* start date is copied back into its late finish date.

Network diagrams are great for sorting out the start and end dates, but not so good at showing what activities are being performed at any one time. The boxes don't always line up as you would want them and, where an activity has float, any decisions you have made to delay the start are not shown.

These difficulties can be overcome by producing a Gantt chart from the network diagram. To do this just draw a horizontal bar for each activity, from its start date to its end date. You can show float if you wish as for B and D in the diagram on the next page.

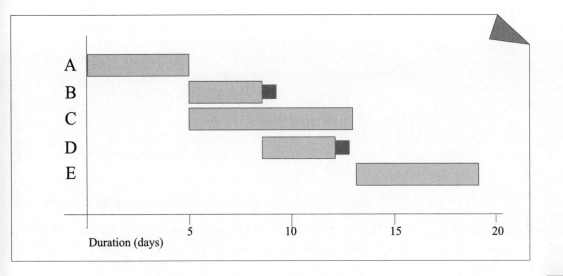

STEP 3: ASSIGN RESOURCES TO THE WORK REQUIRED

As we have said, we cannot treat the people on our project in the same way as our other resources. Each person is an individual, with particular expertise, preferences and approach. Similarly, each activity will require differing combinations of skills and knowledge. The trick here is to identify the expertise required and match it to that which is available.

Alec Rodger has suggested a seven-point plan for use in recruitment. You could use a modified version of this to help you decide whether each activity requires.

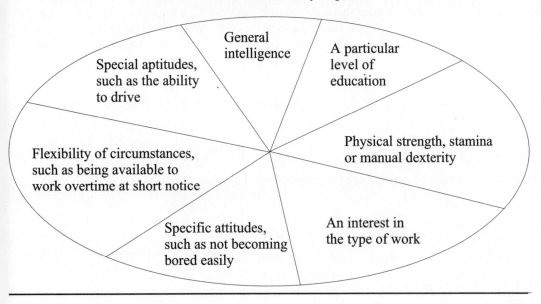

You will then want to identify which of your people best fits the requirements of each job – from personnel records, interviews, the results of tests and so on – so that you can allocate them to appropriate tasks accordingly.

 **Activity**

Use the seven-point plan to identify your own job requirements.

However, life may not be quite as simple as this. You will need to ensure that you can allocate your people sensibly throughout the life of the project so you might wish to give some special attention to *when* they are required, and *how much* they are required.

For example, if you find that you have assigned someone 60 hours work in a week, their over-allocation will cause delays to your project. You may need to reschedule tasks or bring in additional resources. If you have allocated only 20 hours to someone in a week, what will they do for the rest of the time? Is there any other project work you can bring forward – even if it is not critically important?

The process of sorting out all these issues so that people are used in the best way is known as 'resource levelling'. Generally, people want to join a project, do their work and leave. They do not want to be shifted in and out of the project like a yo-yo. Also, if you are bringing in many people, you may not be able to cope with them all at once – or deal with them leaving all at once. These factors tend to suggest that ideally you will aim to recruit people gradually, employ them for a single time span and then redeploy them, gradually reducing your staff toward the end of the project.

The following diagram shows such a profile.

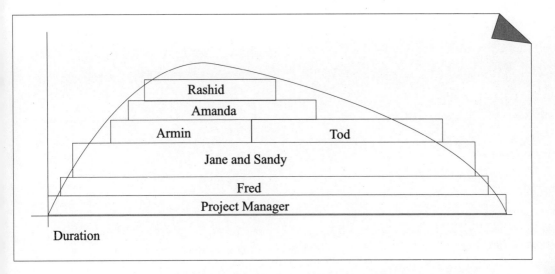

Duration

People are not the only resource you need to level, however.

Similar problems can occur with any limited resource such as equipment. If you need a machine to perform three activities, and all are scheduled at the same time, two will be delayed. If you need something at intervals during the project and it lies idle between, you may find that you are paying (rental charges, for instance) for something you are not using. Can you reschedule your project to improve on this?

By now, you may be wondering how on earth you can balance the needs of the schedule with the needs of staffing and other resource profiling to achieve the best mix. There is no simple method of doing this and even computer programs often fail to produce particularly good results on their own. You may need to use a computer for some of the basic number-crunching and then make manual adjustments to what it produces.

 Fact File

Materials requirement planning (MRP) software uses final production schedules, materials requirements and current stock information to produce scheduling reports and purchasing details all by computer.

However, consider the cost and time of attempting to produce the 'perfect' plan against the cost and time of an imperfect plan. You might find that the imperfect, but quick, plan is a better option.

UNIT 4 | Manage Risks

In this Unit, we will be looking at the risks that can affect your project and how to manage them.

- **Determine what the risks are.**
- **Take action to minimize them.**
- **Be prepared for them.**

Understanding these three actions will help you:

- determine whether you should start the project
- concentrate on the important risks
- take appropriate risk prevention actions
- identify the best people to take ownership of the risks
- identify when a risk is about to occur
- take appropriate curative actions.

Manage risks

STEP 1: IDENTIFY THE RISKS TO YOUR PROJECT

Many organizations especially those which manage projects on a regular basis have formal procedures for identifying and managing risks.

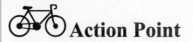 **Action Point**

Are there any formal risk management procedures or risk checklists in your organization? You could look in your:

❖ Project support office
❖ Quality department
❖ Standards department
❖ Library
❖ Where else?

If you find you already have these, assess their relevance to your own situation. Otherwise, you will need to develop your own.

If you do not have procedures or a checklist to help you, you can start to identify risks to your project by looking first at your project assumptions. For example,

In a project that is to create a new product to sell to customers, it has been assumed that the target date of 1 September must be adhered to so as not to miss an important event.

There are risks associated with this assumption, such as the event being cancelled, or moved to August.

Look at each of your assumptions and identify any risks that would change them. Then use each of the following factors to help you identify further risks to your project.

Following on the example, there may be risks that the task is not achievable in the timescale, that a rushed job will result in poor quality, that funds will run dry and so on.

Write each of the risks on the checklist over the page.

Political

Such as attacks on your project from lobby groups and other stakeholders

Technological

Such as those from developing or using 'leading edge' technology

Financial

Such as your project not being allocated the money it needs

People

Such as the possibility of 'human error'

Estimating

Such as caused by inaccuracies

Health & Safety

Such as those caused by the use of dangerous chemicals or machinery

Changes

Such as those imposed on the project's scope or resources

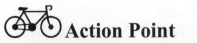 **Action Point**   # Risks

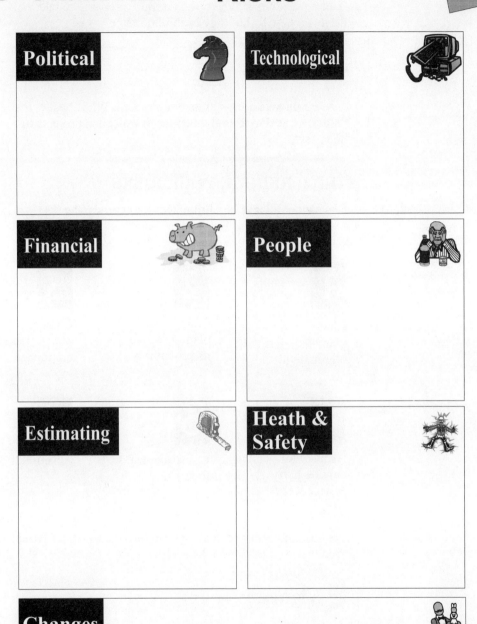

Political	Technological

Financial	People

Estimating	Heath & Safety

Changes

It may also be helpful to identify your organization's approach to risk. How 'risk averse' is it? Would it prefer to take a financial risk or a political risk? Would it prefer to take a technological risk or a people risk? Overall, is it more prepared to take risks with its money, technology or public image?

 Star Tip

You could take a look at its track record. When has it 'stuck its neck out' and when has it cancelled projects in the past?

STEP 2: REDUCE YOUR RISKS

Risks cannot always be eliminated. Sometimes, the best you can do is to trade one risk for another. For each of the risks you have identified, which of the following options is open to you?

1 Change your plan to eliminate it.

2 Change your plan to reduce its probability.

3 Change your plan to reduce its impact.

4 Arrange for another party to accept the risk.

5 Insure against the risk.

6 Accept it.

Is the cost and effort of dealing with the risk worth it? Would it be better to accept the risk?

 Vignette

Many people buy extended warranties to cover the costs of maintaining their new televisions for up to five years, but modern television technology probably means they will not go wrong in that time. It might be better to accept the risk of something going wrong and paying for a repair.

Some people extend this too far, and do not insure their houses. If they get burned to the ground, the cost of replacement is so high that they wish they had paid what suddenly seems a very small insurance premium.

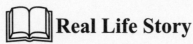 **Real Life Story**

When I worked for a large engineering company a customer was promised delivery on a certain date. After a great deal of scurrying around we managed to produce the materials on time. However, the lorry delivering the material caught fire on the motorway and the whole load had to be re-manufactured. I don't think the customer ever believed the story, although it was absolutely true!

STEP 3: PREPARE CONTINGENT ACTIONS

If, despite your risk reduction activities, a risk should occur, you need to decide what you should do about it.

Look at each risk in turn and decide in outline what you would do. You also need to identify some way of knowing that your contingent action is going to be called for. What should you look out for that will indicate this risk is about to occur?

Now that you have completed your risk assessment exercise, review it and communicate it to anyone who needs to know. This could include anyone on your stakeholder list, but especially anyone who is funding the project or providing resources to it, and anyone who is expecting to receive benefits from it.

You should review your risks periodically throughout the project a subject we shall mention again in Unit 9.

Manage risks

STEP 1: IDENTIFY THE RISKS TO YOUR PROJECT

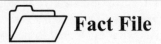 **Fact File**

According to BS6079: Project planning cannot be realistic unless serious account is taken of what could go wrong and what can be done to increase the chances of success and lessen the prospect of partial or complete failure.

Projects are about change. They are also based on assumptions about the future which may or may not turn out to be correct. For these reasons it is important that any project manager identifies the main threats to achievement and devises a plan for dealing with these.

The Fast Track section already includes a list of some useful areas to check for risks. However, it can be difficult to do this in isolation. Apart from the fact that other people can help by sparking off ideas, they may also have information that you do not have, so can bring a new perspective on the analysis. For this reason, risk analysis is best done with others.

Some techniques you can use include:

Brainstorming

Brainstorming in its original sense was a method that allowed unhindered thoughts and many people found the method uncomfortable. You might wish to consider a more restrained form, where completely off-the-wall ideas are not encouraged and where you concentrate on identifying realistic risks.

In the first stage, concentrate on the identification of risks, rather than the assessment or any controlling measures. Only when you have exhausted the process of identification should you attempt to go to the next stage, which is to assess the probability and impact of each risk. We will take that point up shortly.

Expert opinion

Expert opinion is simply seeking the opinions of experts! You might, for example, ask your legal department what could go wrong with contracts. You could ask computer professionals what the technological risks are. You could speak to the accounts department manager and ask what the financial risks are. Each expert might provide you with ideas you would not otherwise have considered. However, their views are likely to be very specific and you will need to decide what weighting to give them in the grand scheme.

Lessons learned

If you can access information about previous projects, you might be able to find out what sorts of risks were considered, and what actually occurred. While your risks may be different, this source of information does enable you to obtain the thoughts and experience of others who are currently inaccessible to you. If the people are still around, you could speak to them as well and get an informal view about what happened.

Which risks matter?

It is likely that some of the risks you identified are trivial. They are not worth pursuing further. Others may be 'showstoppers'. One way of determining which is which is to analyse their probability and impact. Those with a high probability and a high impact are certainly risks to do something about.

Just as with estimating, however, don't make your assessments over precise. They are based on judgement and opinion. It is better to express them in general terms than to assign numbers to them. So, is the probability of each risk high, moderate or low?

If the risk were to occur, would the impact be high, moderate, low or nonexistent for each factor that you consider important such as time, money and quality? (You may recall the point we made in Unit 1 when considering constraints. Ultimately, everything can be expressed in money terms. For this reason, it is often better to omit the money side of risks other than for specific risks to do with procurement, such as price rises. This prevents you from doubling up the impact.)

You can use a simple chart to show the risks, as follows.

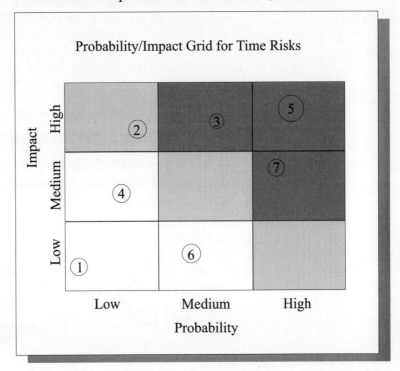

Probability/Impact Grid for Time Risks

In this probability/impact matrix, seven risks have been assessed for their likely impact on time. (Further matrices could be drawn for impacts on other measures, such as cost or quality.)

It would seem that the project manager needs to concentrate on risk 5. Risks 3 and 7 also need close attention. Risk 2 might warrant a short review, but nothing special. Risks 1, 4 and 6 warrant no attention at all. However, they may have an impact in other areas so it is worth logging them just in case.

 **Fact File**

Over the years increasing emphasis has been put on risk assessment in the workplace, often as a result of legislation. A lot of health and safety legislation, for instance, now requires managers to undertake formal risk analyses of their workplace.

Action Point

All managers nowadays have to work within a complex legal framework. You could usefully put together a list of resources that you can use to find out about any legislation that affects you. If you have access to the Internet you will find some pointers at www.open.gov.uk, from where you can access the text of recent Acts of Parliament. Your organization may have a resource centre, or your local library should help.

STEP 2: REDUCE YOUR RISKS

Now that you know which risks to concentrate on, you will want to do something about them. Your choices are to:

Reduce the probability

Reduce the impact

You may be able to do both. You might decide that you can reduce the impact on one measure by increasing it on another, such as taking action to minimize the impact on cost, even though the impact is higher on quality. This will depend on what your project's sensitivities are, which we discussed in Unit 1.

 Fact File

Many buildings at risk of terrorist attack or commercial espionage require high levels of security. There are two basic approaches:

❖ Perimeter security access to the site or the building is closely controlled by guards. Further levels of security are not imposed within the building.

❖ Internal security access to the site or building is monitored. Higher security levels are imposed as required within the building – such as locking away all files, locking internal doors, using visitor IDs and password control to computer systems.

It is not always possible to eliminate a risk entirely. Even if it is, it might not be feasible – perhaps because it costs too much. Any action you take at this point will have an impact on your project, so you need to weigh up the effects carefully. In the Fast Track section, we introduced the idea of insurance paying a definite amount to reduce the *impact* of a risk. (Insurance does not reduce the probability.)

Exercise: How could you reduce the probability and impact of the following risks?

👍 Activity

	To reduce probability	To reduce impact
Losing a key member of staff		
Taking longer than estimated to perform a task		
A supplier is unable to produce the required product		

To reduce the probability of losing a key member of staff, you might ensure that they are motivated, paid adequately and given the types of responsibility they require. To reduce the impact if they should leave, you could ensure that others are able to take on their job – perhaps by training them or, at least, identifying what training they need – and to make sure that you have enough information to recruit a replacement, if there is no-one else available.

To reduce the probability of a task taking longer than estimated, you could ensure that the person doing the job understands the estimate and that they have a plan for achieving the work in that time. To reduce the impact, you could see what scheduling changes could be done to take the task off the critical path, or determine whether parallel activities could be performed, so negating the need to wait for full completion.

To reduce the probability of a supplier being unable to produce the goods, you could ensure that you select the supplier on the basis of ability and track record, that suitable incentives are built in to the contract and that you keep close to the supplier during the work, to check on progress. To reduce the impact, you could see who else could perform the work, find out if partial completion is of any use and investigate the possibility of using a different product instead.

You might also be able to take the other actions we mentioned in Fast Track. However, once you have taken that action and incorporated it into your project plan, you will need to reassess the risks. What risks remain? What are their probabilities? What are their impacts?

 **Action Point**

Draw new probability/impact matrices to reflect your latest analysis.

STEP 3: PREPARE CONTINGENT ACTIONS

For the risks that remain – especially the high probability and high impact risks – you need to consider contingent actions. What will you do if, despite all your good risk management, something happens?

You may be faced with some stark possibilities like scrapping the project, paying the extra money or accepting the delay. However, you may be able to renegotiate with your customer, board or manager, or use a different supplier or reschedule activities.

Whatever options might be open to you, remember that you will only put them into action if the need arises. If you spend a long time preparing detailed contingency plans and the risk doesn't happen, you will have wasted that time. Only work out detailed plans for the high impact risks with moderate or high probability. For example, you might want a plan for recovering from a complete computer systems failure.

For the other risks it is probably better to concentrate on some broad principles what options do you have, which elements of the project are most important and which could be ditched? rather than planning which alternative suppliers to use if a particular consignment fails to arrive.

Finally, risk management is an ongoing process. Review your risks regularly. Delete those that can no longer occur. Add new ones as they arise. That way, if the worst happens, you will be ready for it.

A well-tried and reasonable approach to risk relies on a structured method that takes the following steps:

1 Plan the project, using the techniques we have discussed.

2 Assess the risks associated with the current plan.

3 Determine what changes you can make to eliminate or reduce risks and make those changes.

4 Reassess the risks to determine those that remain and, for each, determine a contingency plan.

5 For each residual risk, determine what will act as a sign that things are going wrong and thus act as a trigger to implement the contingency plan.

6 Ensure that all concerned know about the risks they are taking and accept them.

7 Ensure that you monitor the risks and the warning signs throughout the project.

SKILLBUILDER

Summary of Part I

In this Part, we have covered the actions that generally precede the start of a project.

However, you could consider that each day brings about a new start for the rest of your project. It is therefore necessary to keep revisiting these matters, to see if anything has changed and, if it has, what to do about it. We take up the issues surrounding changes to the project in Unit 9 of Part II.

You should now check through the self assessment checklist we presented at the start of this Part. If you are now confident about these matters, you can go on to Part II. Otherwise, some review of this Part would be useful. The fault-finders that follow have been included to assist you with difficulties you may have at this stage in the project, and you will also be able to use these to extend your general understanding. You may also find the references on the final page of the Workbook helpful, under the heading 'Extending Your Knowledge'.

CHECKPOINT

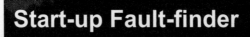

Start-up Fault-finder

At the end of each Part of this Workbook, we have included a fault-finder to help you work out what to do when something is going wrong.

We want you to use the fault-finder to help you think matters through. There is no such thing as 'project management by numbers' and the suggestions will not always work. If this happens, consider whether you are really tackling the problem, or some symptom of a deeper issue. In this respect, people issues are likely to be the most convoluted and complicated ones that you have to deal with and you may need to use several suggestions before you solve the problem.

As with all our checklists, tables and advice, feel free to add your own suggestions – and those you collect from colleagues – to the fault-finder.

Fault-finder

Problem or symptom	Likely cause(s)	Potential action(s)
Cannot get agreement on the scope or objectives of the project.	A. Different stakeholders have different needs.	1. Stakeholders need to form a common view – which they cannot do in isolation. Bring them together in a meeting to discuss the project and allow them to argue the points out. If necessary, keep asking them (jointly) what the scope and objectives of the project are. 2. If agreement cannot be reached, consider whether two (or more) projects might be needed.
	B. There has been insufficient analysis of requirements at a strategic level.	1. Senior managers may simply be unsure of what the project should achieve. Refer them to prior work, such as feasibility studies or research reports. Call a meeting to discuss the issues – perhaps with an expert speaker to help them understand what is needed. 2. It may be necessary to undertake some initial analytical work before the main project begins.
Key stakeholders (such as the customer) will not accept responsibility for their part in the project.	A. They do not understand their importance to the project.	1. Explain to them what the impact will be of their non-involvement. Put it in terms they understand – linking project failure to the failure of their own department's performance. 2. Ask a more senior manager to make the point for you. 3. Ask them to nominate someone to take their place – and make sure that the other person has the authority they require to make decisions and understands the role they need to play.

Fault-finder

Problem or symptom	Likely cause(s)	Potential action(s)
(Continued)	B. They have other pressures that they consider more important.	1. Find out what their other pressures are. You may be able to help alleviate some of them in return for their commitment to your project. You might be able to show that this project is just another pressure and that they need to re-evaluate their priorities. 2. Use pressure yourself – by involving their own manager.
	C. The project is genuinely not as important to them as others believe.	1. Confirm with the others what they think this stakeholder should be responsible for. 2. Call a meeting of all interests to clarify what is really important and what is not. 3. Ask the stakeholder what involvement they would like and whether they are willing to delegate this to someone lower.
	D. There is an undisclosed motivation to continue as they are, without the impact of the project.	1. Your stakeholder table analysis should have picked this one up. Review it. Consider what adverse impact the project might have on this stakeholder. 2. Put yourself in their position. What is so good about the status quo? What is so bad about the new position? 3. Can you change the project's impact to achieve its objectives while allowing this stakeholder to retain their current benefits? Negotiate. Even if you cannot come to an agreement, people are often appreciative of your efforts to involve them and this is often enough to turn an opposer into a supporter.

Fault-finder

Problem or symptom	Likely cause(s)	Potential action(s)
The project will take longer or cost more than management will accept.	A. The estimates are too pessimistic.	1. Review the estimates – using top-down and bottom-up methods. (Never alter the estimates to fit the requirement.) 2. Go through estimates with management and seek common opinions.
	B. Imposed deadlines or budgets are impossible to meet.	1. Ask management what outcomes or deliverables can be dropped from the project. Prioritize the remaining ones and seek to gain acceptance of the high priority items within the limits imposed, with others delivered later if money is available. 2. Seek to split the requirements into more than one project. Management can then prioritize the projects.
Management or customers do not believe the risks and therefore do not take ownership of them.	A. The risks are within their acceptance levels, even if not within yours.	1. Accept that the risks are permissible. 2. Record your concerns in writing – perhaps in a memo.
	B. Your arguments have not been persuasive enough.	1. Review your arguments. Have you watered down a solid argument with lots of small, unconvincing issues? 2. Find out what does concern them and put your arguments in those terms.
	C. You're talking to the wrong person. These are someone else's risks.	1. Find out who really would suffer from the risks you have identified and contact them instead. You may need to get them to explain their concerns to your management.

'Projects are about people'

Making your project happen

By the end of this Part you will be able to:

- determine how to manage your project's progress

- use a systematic approach to solving problems

- understand how to deal with people inside and external to your project

- determine how to ensure an appropriate level of quality

- make decisions about progress, problems, quality and potential changes.

If you are confident that you can already answer 'Yes' to most or all of the following questions you might like simply to refresh your memory by scanning the Fast Track pages in each Unit and then move on to Part III.

Self assessment checklist: Part 1	
I am confident that I can:	**Yes ☑ No ☒**
Determine objectively the project's progress and take the necessary action.	
Solve problems associated with mysteries, difficulties and dilemmas.	
Motivate people within the project team and set appropriate goals.	
Influence those people outside the project when their involvement is required.	
Define an appropriate quality environment.	
Instigate processes leading to quality products and check the effectiveness of them.	
Deal with changes to the project brought about by internal and external pressures.	

UNIT 5 Manage Progress

In this Unit, we will be covering the steps you need to take when managing progress in your project.

- **Define measures for progress-checking.**
- **Instigate methods of control.**
- **Instigate a method of reporting.**

Understand these three steps will help you:

- recognise how your project is progressing and measure it objectively
- decide what to do when progress is not adequate
- take control so as to ensure the project moves on
- make others aware of progress and gain their support when needed.

Manage progress

STEP 1: DEFINE MEASURES FOR PROGRESS-CHECKING

Progress-checking is a vital task. However, you will only be able to measure your progress if you know what to measure and what to compare it against. You first task must therefore be to decide what you can measure to test progress against your plan.

Your plan will probably take account of three particular constraints – cost, outcomes (or quality) and time. What will you measure against each of these?

For example, in Lucy's project to plan a conference, she knows what outcomes have to be achieved by which dates, to meet her deadline. She could check off outcome completion on those dates to see if she is on schedule. For long activities, she could check partway through by asking how much more work needs to be done to complete the activity.

Note that Lucy will not ask how much work has been done to date for the longer activities. This is historical fact, but not much use for checking whether she is on time. People tend to suggest that things are going well, even when they are not. What is important is to know how much longer she will have to wait.

Action Point

Now decide on your own progress monitors. What will you measure and when? Complete the following form.

	What to measure	When to measure it
Outcomes		
Cost		

STEP 2: INSTIGATE METHODS OF CONTROL

Now that you have decided what to measure and when, you need to find out how to control progress to make your project meet its time, cost and outcome objectives. The action you need to take will be based upon the monitoring your have performed.

For example, in Lucy's project, she expected the whole list of speakers to be ready by 4 June, prior to printing the publicity leaflets. It is now 30 May and two speakers have yet to confirm the engagement. That, so far, is monitoring. Lucy can now take controlling action by asking her assistant, Ben, to telephone the two speakers and ask them to fax their confirmation, and to look for alternative speakers, just in case.

At the start of each project and at the start of each activity take action to ensure that the project stays on track. Ensure that people know what is expected of them – what outcome you expect, how long they have got and possibly how much money they have to spend. Check progress before it's too late – not when the outcome is supposed to have been completed.

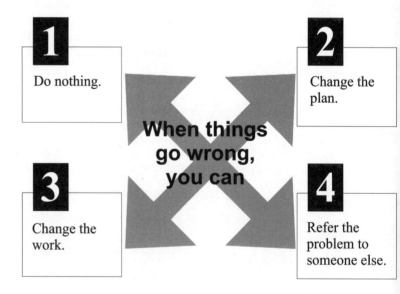

1 Do nothing.

2 Change the plan.

When things go wrong, you can

3 Change the work.

4 Refer the problem to someone else.

Your job, as project manager, is to decide which is most appropriate.

If progress is being affected by changes to the project's requirements, or unexpected problems, refer to the risk plans you developed in Unit 4 and look at Unit 9 for advice on managing change.

STEP 3: INSTIGATE A METHOD OF REPORTING

You also need to decide when to report on progress.

Too frequently and you will demotivate your team who will resent your intrusion.

Too infrequently and you will miss the points where action needs to be taken.

Look back at your project plan. Did you identify a critical path? For these activities, you need to keep a close control. For others, you can afford to stand back a bit.

Look at your risk plan. Did you identify things to look out for, that will give you an indication of a risk occurring? For these, you will also need to monitor more frequently.

Use 'checkpoints' – time-based reporting points where everyone reports progress and provides information so you can review the project against the plan.

Use exception reporting where you assume that everything is proceeding to plan unless told otherwise.

Consider how and when your own manager wants to be kept informed. This may guide you as to when to do your own evaluation of progress, so that you can pass on up-to-date information and any plan revisions.

1

What reports should you produce?

2

When should you produce these?

Check List   **Progress Control**

Project name: Report date:

What we should have completed by now but have not:

What we have completed ahead of schedule:

What we now need to complete in the next reporting period:

Potential delay to whole project:

Potential overspend:

Potential shortfall in quality or functionality:

New risks identified:

Risks deleted:

**YOU MAY NOW CONTINUE WITH THE NEXT UNIT ON PAGE 95
OR MOVE TO THE SKILLBUILDER SECTION THAT FOLLOWS**

Manage progress

STEP 1: DEFINE MEASURES FOR PROGRESS-CHECKING

 **Fact File**

A recent (1996) study reports the counterintuitive fact that in order to keep a project within budget, the project manager should NOT use cost as a controlling mechanism but should, instead, concentrate on the time schedule. If the project comes in on time, the costs will be within budget.

In fact, time itself is something that does not need measuring. What you should measure are your outcomes and your costs against the time base. You may then need to reappraise your time estimate for duration of the project.

Progress monitoring

 Activity

The best way to gauge progress is to see what activities are currently taking place.

 True

 False

The most obvious way of determining progress is to look at the outcomes completed so far and compare these to the plan. If you constructed a Product Flow Diagram, this will help you to determine what your progress is to date. You can also look at your network diagram or Gantt chart, if you can identify on them what outcomes should have been produced.

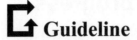

Guideline

Measure completed work only. It is not wise to attempt to measure progress by looking at activities. For a start, it can be misleading to take the view that, as half the time has been taken up, half the progress has been made. Often, things come together suddenly at the end and intermediate measures do not reflect this. On the other hand, a particularly difficult piece of work may be left to the end and so delay an activity that, up to now, has been going just fine.

Also, people have a nasty habit of telling you that the work is 80 per cent complete, whatever its real status. These factors, combined with your original estimates, themselves of dubious accuracy, will prevent you from getting an accurate picture.

It is therefore better to break the project down into products (as we suggested earlier) and tick them off on your plan only when they are completed.

For incomplete products, you can ask the person responsible for a new estimate of the time they now need to complete the task. This gives you a much better picture of the future needs of your project.

 Star Tip

Involving people in agreeing their own deadlines gives them some ownership, which leads to motivation for them to complete by the date they said.

Cost monitoring

Whether it is top priority or not it is likely that your organization will want you to undertake some form of budget management. You will therefore need to keep at least the basic records of money in and out and be able to provide an audit trail for later investigation. It is also imperative that you understand the behaviour of the costs of your project. It can be all too easy to cut costs in one area to save money and find that this causes higher costs somewhere else. It seems to be a strange fact that there is never enough money to do a job properly, but money can always be found to clear up the mess at twice the cost or more.

 **Activity**

Examine the financial systems operating for your own project.

* ❖ How well do they meet your own and your organization's information requirements?
* ❖ Is the information timely?
* ❖ How can you use it to improve on your forecasting?

It can also be good to develop some idea about the cost of the various tasks or outputs associated with your project. By knowing how much a product or service should cost you are in a good position to identify when actual costs exceed this and hence when things are going wrong. You can do this by using a process known as variance analysis.

 Case Study

Future Perfect Training is undertaking a project to accredit candidates for a number of National Vocational Qualifications (NVQs). An NVQ assessment might typically require 10 hours' assessment time, an allowance for travel costs, an hour for verification plus awarding body registration and certification fees.

The standard costs of assessment would therefore be:

Registration and certification:	£45
Assessment 10 hours @ £25/hr:	£250
Travel 20 miles @ 25p:	£5
Verification 1 hour @ £30:	£30
Standard cost:	£330

If a subsequent assessment actually cost £335 the training manager could analyse the reason for the extra cost, and use the results to improve control or inform future planning.

Before you turn the page, think through some reasons why this assessment might have cost extra.

SKILLBUILDER

Case Study (continued)

Further analysis shows that the actual costs were:

Registration and certification:	£45
Assessment 9 hours @ £25/hr:	£225
Travel 60 miles @ 25p:	£15
Verification 2 hours @ £25:	£50
Actual cost:	£335

The variances are therefore:

Assessment: 1 hour less than expected a gain of £25
Travel: 40 miles more than expected a loss of £10
Verification: 1 hour more than expected at a price of £5/hr less – a loss overall of £30

Making a total (unfavourable) variance of £5

Variances from plan can be as a result of:

❖ using more or less of a resource than expected
❖ paying a higher or lower cost than expected.

 Activity

Which variance is which in *Future Perfect Training*'s case?

	More/less resource	Higher/lower cost
Assessment		
Travel		
Verification		

Assessment = less resource
Travel = more resource
Verification = more resource at lower cost

This type of analysis can help you identify those differences that you can do something about – such as those to do with performance and those you just have to accept – such as price fluctuations.

Whatever you do to manage it, however, progress control starts with planning. After all, as Alice found out from the Cheshire Cat, if you don't know where you want to get to it doesn't much matter which way you go!

STEP 2: INSTIGATE METHODS OF CONTROL

In the Fast Track section, we said that you can change the plan or change the work, refer on or do nothing. Your choice will depend on whether you need to take action and, if you do, what you want to achieve.

Do nothing

This is the choice to take when you can see that the work is going just fine. It is also the choice to take when you expect the work to fit reasonably closely to the plan in the medium to longer term, even though it is ahead of or behind schedule right now.

Refer on

You will need to do this if the problem lies outside the area or level of your responsibility. Your manager or the project board will probably appreciate a recommendation on what to do, however, so you may benefit from considering the following two options anyway.

Change the plan

If the work is just fine and you can now see that the plan is inaccurate, you might be tempted to do this. Beware! This makes it difficult to measure the project's success easily as it can hide all sorts of problems. Project auditors are well used to seeing changes to project plans and home in on them as a possible source of hidden errors. However, it might be a sensible option (keeping a record of the previous version) to ensure that the rest of the project benefits from the updates. You will certainly need to do this if it has been subjected to changes – but more of that in Unit 9.

Change the work

That leaves this as the final option. In fact, it can mean changing either the nature of the job or how it is being performed. For example, you could alter the quality criteria, reduce functionality or seek an alternative product. You could also speak to the people involved and try to get them to work faster, take fewer breaks, chat less, do some overtime or concentrate more so that fewer errors are made. The choices here are numerous and often the part of project management that lets the rest of it down by not being done at all.

In fact, very often the main problems in a project are human.

Activity

Have a look at the following situations and see what solutions you can think of.

❖ Susan is spending too much time on unimportant aspects of the job
❖ Paul is making a lot of mistakes
❖ Rav seems to spend more time around the coffee machine than at his desk
❖ Julie is new and seems to underestimate the amount of work in hand
❖ Sally and Kate seem unable to get on with each other and their work is suffering
❖ Hetty and Tom are married to each other and each has a heavy workload in the project, which is slipping behind time

Susan

Make sure that Susan knows what to produce. Give her a Product Description or a specification. Make sure she knows the quality criteria and how these will be measured.

Paul

Make sure that Paul has the skills, knowledge and attitudes to do the job. Refer back to Unit 4 for more information on this. If he doesn't, can you

- ❖ train him
- ❖ coach him
- ❖ get him to work with someone else who does
- ❖ replace him
- ❖ work alongside him

Rav

Make sure he knows what the priorities are.

- ❖ When does the job have to be done by?
- ❖ Why is that?

Find out if he has enough to do – he may simply be bored.

Julie

Give Julie intermediate reporting points. Don't wait until the last moment before checking progress. Ask to see a plan of her work (produced by her) and then a draft. Not only does this give you advance notice of problems, it acts as a motivator for Julie and shows her how important the task is to you.

Sally and Kate

If they work in a team, make sure the team leader knows how to motivate them.

- ❖ What team pressures are on them?
- ❖ Will these help or hinder?
- ❖ Can they be changed, reduced or reinforced?

> ### Hetty and Tom
>
> Find out what other pressures they have at work or at home. Make timescales reasonable given the other demands on their time and attention. Consider splitting the job to suit. Most people will respond positively to attempts to fit the job around their needs.

Generally speaking, if you are not satisfied with what your staff are doing, you need to tell them.

- ❖ Keep it private and keep it factual.
- ❖ Direct your comments at their activities, not at them personally. Rather than 'You're a slow worker', say 'It does not look like the work will be ready on time'. You might make similar comments about the quality 'There are 15 mistakes on this page. That is too many'.
- ❖ Ask them to suggest what they can do about it. It is more powerful for them to suggest the way forward than for you to impose your own plan.

Finally, be aware that *you* might be the cause of any problem!

- ❖ Do you say one thing and do another?
- ❖ Do you give two people the same job to do, without telling either?
- ❖ Do you impose your own ideas and deny those of others?
- ❖ Do you denigrate efforts of others – especially in public?

If so, review your behaviour and replace these traits with the suggestions we have given instead.

>  **Star Tip**
>
> If they have to implement them, your team's mediocre ideas will always work a lot better than your brilliant ones!

Of course, people will not cause you problems all of the time. If you are satisfied with what they are doing, tell them. Don't make a song and dance about it. A simple 'Well done' or 'That's coming on fine' will suffice.

STEP 3: INSTIGATE A METHOD OF REPORTING

In addition to your informal, individual monitoring, you will also need a formal method of reporting. This will help you to collect statistical data about the project and document progress. This, in turn, will aid your decision-making and support your decisions in future project reviews.

You need to consider both the reports that you need to receive and those you need to pass upwards. Here, we introduce the idea of Checkpoints and Highlights – concepts from the PRINCE method.

Checkpoints

PRINCE uses checkpoints as a basic form of collecting data about progress and requirements. You can hold checkpoints at what ever interval you decide, but intervals of one to two weeks is common.

The idea behind a checkpoint is to enable you, as the Project Manager, to collect information about those products that are finished and those that are in progress. Whilst this often takes place at a meeting you don't have to do things this way.

One model that you might like to adopt splits the checkpoint into three elements:

1

Data collection: this involves project staff completing time-sheets showing how much work they have undertaken during the checkpoint period so that you get some idea of the interaction of time, cost and outputs. You should also ask your staff to estimate what further time they think they will need on each product and to highlight any likely problems during the next checkpoint period.

2

Information collation: to provide you with a clear idea of the actual costs and expected future costs of each product under development. You will need to highlight whether the products are likely to be completed on time and to budget and, if not, what your revised estimates are. This will enable you to produce projections which are based on something more than simply an idle guess.

Decision-making: a meeting between you as project manager, project support staff, the team leaders and others who need to be involved, to discuss the issues that have been raised and resolve problems. You can use these meetings to discuss allocations of people over the next checkpoint period and beyond. In this way the checkpoint develops into a means of real control, changing things to make them happen.

Highlight reports

You will prepare and send these at intervals to your manager or Project Board. The idea behind highlight reports is to keep management informed about progress since they are not involved in your project on a day to day basis. You would normally send a copy to each relevant manager individually, to a format agreed with them in advance or maybe to comply with organizational standards.

Charts or graphs are ideal for showing an overall impression and can be supplemented with some basic figures, such as money spent, if necessary. Here is an example, showing typical headings.

Highlight Report for project Alpha
Period 12

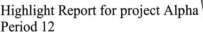

Spend profile

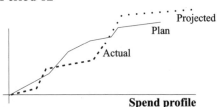

Variances

Currently Projected Completion
Date   23 August
Cost   £234 000

Explanation of Progress to Date

Progress has been marred by difficulties with outside contractors. However, these have now been solved and progress is picking up. Inevitably the project will be later completing than planned.

Explanation of Variances

Due to the reasons outlined above, the project is now two months late. This has caused additional costs to employ project staff and we are paying extra for a higher quality product, as approved.

Matters for Management Attention

Customers will need to be informed of the late delivery of the new service.

Support staff training will be put back by about two weeks.

UNIT 6 — Solve Problems and Make Decisions

In this Unit, we will be covering the actions you need to take when you have a problem.

- **Define it.**
- **Deal appropriately with it.**

Understanding these actions will help you:

- differentiate between different types of problem
- define appropriate solutions
- decide which solution to take.

Solve problems and make decisions

STEP 1: DEFINE THE PROBLEM

When you find that your project is not proceeding according to plan you have a problem. A large part of project management is to do with identifying problems and taking decisions about them. The first step when this occurs is to decide whether or not the problem is a symptom of something else. If it is you need to decide which you should tackle. For example:

Charities that concentrate on providing shelter for homeless people often find that their client groups have a number of associated problems. These will range from drug or alcohol addiction to the contracting of dangerous diseases. These problems may well have come about as a result of someone leaving home at an early age. This may have been the result of childhood abuse. The problem of homelessness can therefore be tackled at any one of a number of levels and many charities have to define their roles carefully in order to avoid 'butterflying' between problems and their causes.

 **Action Point**

Analyse the problem you are facing at the moment and summarize what you need to solve in about six to a dozen words.

My problem is:

Your next step is to decide what sort of problem it is.

Mystery	**Difficulty**	**Dilemma**
Mystery – where there is potentially a 'correct' solution such as the reason (or reasons) for a machine breakdown	Difficulty – where you are lacking the resources to achieve what's required	Dilemma – where you are dependent on something you cannot know like what interest rates will be like in 12 months' time

You will need to tackle these different sorts of problem in different ways by painstaking analysis in the case of a mystery, by identifying alternative ways of achieving your aim in the case of a difficulty or by limiting your risk in the case of a dilemma.

 **Action Point**

Is your current problem a:

❖ Mystery
❖ Difficulty
❖ Dilemma

How will you go about tackling it?

STEP 2: DEAL APPROPRIATELY WITH DIFFERENT TYPES OF DECISION

Once you have identified what your problem is you are in a much better position to make a decision about how to solve it. Before you do this, however, you will want to find out what options you have. This will depend partly on the type of decision required. For example, the decisions needed to solve mystery type problems should be relatively straightforward once you have identified the cause. Difficulties and dilemmas require more thought in terms of what your objectives are and what alternatives are open to you.

 **Action Point**

What do you want to achieve as a result of this decision?

What options look likely to meet this need?

Having generated your options you then need to decide how you will determine which option to go for. You will do this by deciding on any essential and desirable criteria. For example:

Gerda was the senior nurse in a private hospital. She had been asked to undertake a project to find ways of reducing the vast amount of paperwork stored in the roof space, which had to be kept for legal reasons but which represented a fire hazard and was impossible to access. Having undertaken a lot of research she recommended the purchase of a computerized document imaging system which would eliminate the need for paper records and make access quick and efficient. However, her solution was rejected on cost grounds and she was sent away to identify a cheaper if less beneficial option.

Gerda made several mistakes here, not least in failing to clarify the cost constraints of her project. Nevertheless, if she had identified and perhaps lobbied her stakeholders more effectively she might still have had more success. In your own situation you will need to identify the essential and desirable criteria that your decision must meet and also any potential objections that you need to overcome. As an interim measure, are there any steps that you can take in a particular direction without committing yourself too much?

 **Action Point**

How will you communicate your decision and to whom?

What support do you need for your decision?

Is it possible to delay the decision or perhaps to take small steps that do not commit you too far?

Finally, if your decision has long-term implications you will need to review it from time to time in order to ensure that it is still sensible to proceed.

 **Action Point**

Is it appropriate to review the decision?

When?

YOU MAY NOW CONTINUE WITH THE NEXT UNIT ON PAGE 109 OR MOVE TO THE SKILLBUILDER SECTION THAT FOLLOWS

FAST TRACK

Solve problems and make decisions

STEP 1: DEFINE THE PROBLEM

As we saw in Fast Track, there are different types of problem.
While there are also several different systems in use for
classifying them, the one I tend to use defines problems in terms
of whether they are:

Mysteries

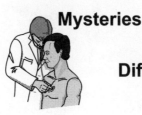

Difficulties

Dilemmas

Mystery

A mystery is perhaps the archetypal problem. Something unexpected happens – the car breaks down, or the milk isn't delivered as usual. What has gone wrong? What is different about today?

Difficulty

A difficulty might occur when you know what you would like, or need, to do but don't have the means (the physical, mental or emotional resources) to achieve it. I may want to be an astronaut, for instance, but I face a few difficulties on the way.

Dilemma

A dilemma, on the other hand, represents the sort of situation where it is impossible to know what to do next. Either we just don't have the information we need to decide, or there seem to be so many bad points to all our options that it seems that we would be jumping out of the frying pan and into the fire.

Real Life Story

Recently my seven-year-old car broke down. Its gearbox had to be replaced. Having spent several hundred pounds on it, I faced a dilemma. Should I now sell it, in the expectation that something else equally as expensive might break down, or keep it a bit longer in an effort to get my money's worth out of the repair?

(I actually decided to keep it. Within six weeks it was back at the garage having a new computer installed!)

Each of these 'problem' situations demands a different approach, each of which depends on the acquisition and use of information.

 **Activity**

How might you classify each of the following types of problem? How might you go about solving them?

a) I have switched on my television but there is no picture on the screen

b) Your receptionist has called in sick and there is nobody to replace him on the front desk

c) You have double-booked yourself and need to be in two different meetings at the same time

I would classify them as follows:

❖ Problem 'a' is a mystery, which you cannot solve until you know the facts
❖ Problem 'b' is a difficulty you are lacking a vital resource
❖ Problem 'c' is a dilemma you cannot know in advance which of the two meetings will prove the more worthwhile

Here are some Guidelines for examining each of these problem types.

The mystery

⤷ Guideline

You cannot solve a mystery until you know the facts. You need to find what is distinctive about the mystery: its location, identity, time and extent.

Ask 'When does it occur?' 'When does it NOT occur?' 'When did it first occur?' 'Where does it occur?' 'Where does it NOT occur?' 'What is different now…?' and so forth.

⤷ Guideline

Document the situation (in a grid or other scheme to draw out a picture) to pinpoint the problem.

⤷ Guideline

Generate possible causes, then compare each possible cause against the known effects.

To be a good candidate cause it must account for every effect and must not generate effects that you have not identified.

⤷ Guideline

Investigate more fully the possible causes that seem most likely – to home in on the actual cause.

So, in the television example, I might find that this is the first time that I have lost the picture; that the television worked well last night when I used it last; that there is no sound either; that there was no 'hum' when I pressed the 'on' button and that if I press the button again still nothing happens. The only thing that is different this time is that I have vacuumed the room this morning. Possible causes might be a transmission fault, electrical problems or the breakdown of a mechanical part. However, a transmission fault would not account for the lack of response when I switched the television on but an electrical fault would – and so would a mechanical fault with the button itself. Given my cleaning activities, however, the most likely cause is that I have forgotten to replace the plug after using the socket for the vacuum cleaner. I investigate that possibility find that this is true, replace the plug and the television works again.

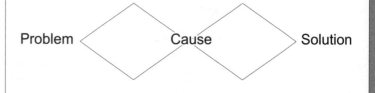
There are techniques available to help with generating the possible causes of mystery type problems. You may remember that we looked at 'brainstorming' in Unit 4. Another technique is known as the 'fishbone' or Ishikawa diagram (named after its inventor). A fishbone diagram displays all possible causes of the problem stemming from a central line (the fishbone). Each of these causes can then be investigated in more detail by asking 'Why?' repeatedly until no further progress can be made.

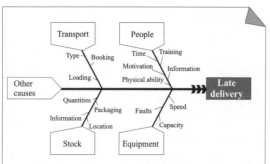

In this example of using a fishbone diagram the problem relates to the late delivery of pizzas. The potential reasons for the problem have been identified as:

❖ Equipment
❖ Stock
❖ People
❖ Transport
❖ Other

Each of these has been split into a number of component parts. There could be a problem to do with the equipment breaking down, for instance, or it may simply not be up to the job. Each of these components can then be investigated systematically and the main causes of the problem highlighted and dealt with.

You will see that the process of compiling a fishbone diagram can help you to decide at what level to tackle your problem.

The difficulty

Remember that, with a difficulty, you are lacking a vital resource. In order to solve it:

 **Guideline**

State exactly what you are trying to achieve.

 **Guideline**

State the difficulty in terms of what prevents you from advancing: lack of resources (internal such as willpower or external such as money).

 **Guideline**

Investigate ways of achieving your goal without the resource you lack. (This could be an altogether different approach to the one you have been trying.) Identify others who may be able to supply the resource you lack or who may be able to assist with generating alternative approaches.

 **Guideline**

If the difficulty still exists, investigate ways of obtaining the resource you lack and the cost of obtaining it. (Cost may not be in money terms: obtaining something you want may cost you time or emotional stress.)

In the sick receptionist example in the earlier quiz, you may decide that you want to ensure that visitors are welcomed and attended to when they arrive at the building. Is it possible to do this without the receptionist? Alternatives might include:

❖ asking another member of staff to take over
❖ leaving a note in reception
❖ asking visitors to dial your extension on arrival
❖ hiring a temporary member of staff.

The most effective solution will be the one which most closely matches your requirements in terms of required results and constraints. If you have other staff available who can carry out their normal work, or at least part of it, whilst staffing the desk then this would be an obvious way forward. If you are not in this position but do have a budget for temps then this might be your preferred solution. The message here is that, without clarifying your objectives and constraints, you are making it much more difficult for yourself to achieve an optimum result.

The dilemma

With a dilemma you really do not know which alternative to choose. When you face a dilemma you therefore need to:

Be very clear about your objectives: short and long term. There may be conflicts between the two.

Look for commonality between your objectives. Is there a compromise? Is there a later point when you could alter your decision, so that you can make an interim decision now and move on?

Can you collect any further information to help in your decision?

Can you identify any parallel decisions (perhaps made by others, or made by you in the past) that may guide your thoughts?

In the meetings example in the quiz above, you might decide to look at the aims and agenda for each meeting.

- ❖ Who will be there?
- ❖ What are the implications of your non-attendance?
- ❖ Is there anyone else who could stand in for you?
- ❖ Who could you approach?
- ❖ Have you attended any similar meetings which have been a waste of time or really useful?

STEP 2: DEAL APPROPRIATELY WITH DIFFERENT TYPES OF DECISION

If you remember, in Step 1 we identified a number of questions which should help to determine both the nature of a problem and the likely solutions to it.

However, once we have identified the possible solutions we need to make a decision about which – if any – to choose.

Dealing with a mystery

Very often, once the mystery has been diagnosed, you know what to do and the decision is straightforward. In other cases, you may find yourself faced with a different problem – a difficulty or a dilemma. If so, study that problem using the information we gave in Step 1, then follow it up with the advice below.

Dealing with a difficulty

As difficulties are about a lack of resource, your only ways of dealing with them are:

- ❖ Find the resource
- ❖ Find an alternative resource
- ❖ Focus on a different outcome

Not all three of these may be available to you and you need to be prepared to accept the 'different outcome' of doing nothing about it! However, you can keep the problem in mind – you might be able to tackle it later.

This is one of those times when the support of your stakeholders can be useful. Can they provide the resource you need? If the difficulty is caused by one of their requirements, are they willing to reduce or alter the requirement?

In the meantime, you may need to refer the problem upwards to your manager.

Dealing with a dilemma

Dilemmas are where you can only take one course of action and you cannot determine which to take. These are the ones that catch out many people and result in procrastination.

If it is likely that there will be little difference in effect between your possible actions, then it doesn't matter which one you choose. Flip a coin and take that route.

If you flip a coin and don't want to take that option, the process will at least have made you aware of your own innermost feelings on the matter. You don't have to go with the coin – choose the other option if you are more comfortable with it.

If you feel that your decision will have more serious consequences, can you delay the decision? Can you involve other people to get a different angle on the decision and gauge their views?

Can you take a partial decision now, see how things go and make a further decision later? If you cannot, you are faced with the stark prospect of choosing between two options with insufficient information about either and no way of differentiating. On that basis, no one can blame you for whichever option you take. Just go for one of them and make the best of it. However bad things get, you will never know how much worse it could have been with the other choice – and neither will anyone else!

 Fact File

An item in the 28 August 1997 edition of Computer Weekly stated that:

'Involving staff in decisions, either directly or through consultation schemes, benefits their employers, according to a European Commission study. The biggest impact is on quality: more than 90% of the 5,800 European employers surveyed reported definite improvement from staff involvement. Just over 80% of employers now have some form of staff consultation.'

UNIT 7 | Work Effectively with Your People

In this Unit, we will be looking at ways of motivating your team and others who have an influence over it. It will cover how to:

- **Motivate your team and set goals.**
- **Influence those who are outside the team.**

Understanding these actions will help you:

- understand how to motivate different individuals according to their need
- understand how to supervise them appropriately
- negotiate with people about what needs to be done, when by and to what quality
- ensure that those outside the project are kept informed and involved as needed.

Work effectively with your people

STEP 1: MOTIVATE YOUR TEAM AND SET GOALS

We have already seen that many of the problems you will face as a project manager will stem from people issues. To get the best out of your team you first need to gather a few facts about the individuals concerned – in particular, who they are, what their capabilities and experience are and what is likely to interest and motivate them.

For example:

A team member who is keen, willing but inexperienced is likely to need more background information when being given instructions than an experienced old hand. However, that same old hand may have lost her enthusiasm for the job and you may need to discuss with her the challenges she is seeking to rekindle her interest and enthusiasm.

Now think through the members of your project team and answer the questions below. You may like to photocopy this page before completing the form, to keep it confidential.

Action Point

Who reports to you?	What is likely to motivate them?	How much supervision do they need?	How will you motivate and supervise them?

You will also need to look at your product or work breakdown structure and resource plans to determine who should undertake what tasks, and when. You will want to agree these tasks, where appropriate, in the form of objectives. In general – and where possible – you will want to agree 'outcome' objectives with your staff. These are objectives phrased in terms of end results, as opposed to process objectives, which define how the task should be tackled. Exceptions to this rule might be with new staff or those whose performance is causing you concern. Either way, your objectives will need to be SMART.

- ❖ Specific
- ❖ Measurable
- ❖ Achievable
- ❖ Relevant
- ❖ Time bound

 **Action Point**

Looking at your list above, decide the type of objectives you should normally agree with each member of your team – process or outcome.

How can you ensure that the targets you agree are SMART?

 **Action Point**

Think about a project area that you would like to delegate. Plan your approach, using the checklist on the next page.

✓ Checklist

Part of project to delegate:	
Who to delegate to:	
Why this person is most suitable for this part of the project:	
What outcomes they are to produce:	
What they need to do to achieve these outcomes:	
How to ensure that they have understood what they need to do and to achieve:	
The support or encouragement they require:	

STEP 2: INFLUENCE THOSE WHO ARE OUTSIDE THE TEAM

In Unit 1 we spent some time identifying and analysing the different stakeholders in your project. Review the work you did then and make sure you can answer the following questions:

Using the analysis you produced in Unit 1, answer the following questions in relation to your own project's stakeholders.

🚲 Action Point

Who else do you need to work through to achieve your project's aims?	
Are they for, against or neutral to the project?	
How will you influence them?	
How much chasing do they need?	
What information do they need to receive about the project?	
In what format should this be?	
When should you update them?	

YOU MAY NOW CONTINUE WITH THE NEXT UNIT ON PAGE 123
OR MOVE TO THE SKILLBUILDER SECTION THAT FOLLOWS

Work effectively with your people

STEP 1: MOTIVATE YOUR TEAM AND SET GOALS

 Fact File

David Kirk, captain of the successful New Zealand All Blacks rugby team, provides us with the following five pointers for successful team work:

❖ Valuing members as individuals
❖ Integrating people within the team
❖ As leader, being fair with everyone
❖ Instilling a sense of confidence in the team
❖ Encouraging enjoyment

Membership of a team can be particularly satisfying for those people with strong 'affiliation' needs at work.

The need for affiliation is just one of three needs identified by psychologist David McClelland during his research in the 1950s and 1960s. Other people have more of a need to exercise power, others have a need for achievement. This has implications for you as a manager endeavouring to get the best out of your staff. Asking a person with strong affiliation needs to work on a task alone is unlikely to bring out the best in them. Asking someone who has a strong need to achieve and 'do a good job' to skimp on quality is likely to lead to resentment and demotivation. So, while you may well be trying to encourage the individuals in your team to work well together, you also need to treat each person as an individual and take account of his personal characteristics.

 Activity

This example is just one from innumerable theories of motivation that have been suggested over the years. What other theories of motivation have you come across? See if you can pair up the right name with the right theory!

Maslow	Hackman and Oldham
Locke and Latham	Herzberg

Hierarchy of needs	Motivators and hygiene factors
Goal setting	Variety, identity, significance, autonomy, feedback

115

Maslow

A long time ago Abraham Maslow produced his 'hierarchy of needs' – based on the need to satisfy low level needs such as job security before higher level ones such as job satisfaction.

Herzberg

Fred Herzberg found that a number of factors affected people's satisfaction levels at work (motivators and 'hygiene' factors) and this led him to advocate job enrichment as a good way of motivating staff.

Hackman and Oldham

More recently, Hackman and Oldham have developed this approach and suggest that the most motivating jobs all contain certain features. These are:

❖ Skill variety – the extent to which the work requires a range of skills
❖ Task identity – the extent to which the work provides a whole, identifiable outcome
❖ Task significance – the extent to which the work has an impact on others (or possibly on themselves)
❖ Autonomy – the extent of choice and discretion
❖ Feedback from the job – the extent to which the work itself provides feedback on how well it is being performed

These features have implications for the way in which you divide up tasks and responsibilities between members in your team. However, the need for strong control in some projects or task areas can somewhat offset the advantages of variety, identity and significance. How can you, as a project manager, implement effective controls without your staff feeling that you are 'breathing down their necks' all the time?

Locke and Latham

Part of the answer might come from the work of Locke and Latham, who suggest that people are motivated by having difficult but achievable goals but only in so far as they have had a real say in agreeing them. In particular, they suggest that goals should be specific rather than general ('do your best') and that they should be provided with regular feedback on how they are doing.

This fits in neatly with the idea of agreeing 'SMART' objectives. We have seen that 'SMART' objectives are:

S pecific – do they clarify precisely what they are about?

M easurable – how will you know when they have been achieved?

A chievable – are they within the authority and control of your member of staff?

R elevant – are they to do with important parts of the job the 'critical success factors' or 'key result areas'?

T imebound – have you agreed over what period they should be achieved? Are there any other time constraints that you should include?

 **Activity**

But what does this mean in practice? Have a look at the following objectives and see how 'SMART' you think they are.

	S	M	A	R	T
1. To have worked through this Unit by the end of the month					
2. To have improved John's absence record before the start of the busy season					
3. To have reduced average customer waiting time from ten to nine minutes by the end of next year.					

As far as the first objective is concerned, it is reasonably measurable, and presumably achievable, relevant and timebound. However, you may well have thought – and I would agree – that it is not particularly specific. What is it that needs to be achieved here? Presumably the person going through the Unit has some reason for doing so. If they were to clarify this to themselves it would help them to make the best use of their time and ensure that they got what they wanted from their efforts.

The second objective may well be relevant and it is also timebound – but again is not very specific. What constitutes an 'improvement' and over what period of time? However, the main problem with this objective is the fact that the person who needs to achieve it is not necessarily in a position to do so. Certainly, there may be actions that John's manager could take to improve his attendance, but if John has genuine problems she may be unable to resolve them.

The final objective is specific, measurable and timebound and could well be achievable. To that extent, it is 'SMART'. However, it does not sound to be very stretching and so may well not be as relevant as it could be. That may or may not be a problem, but would certainly be worth investigating a little

 Activity

Now have a go at rephrasing these objectives to make them more 'SMART'.

1. To have …

2. To have …

3. To have …

further.

My ideas would be:

1. To have picked up three ways of encouraging team members and stakeholders to pull together to achieve the project's aims by the end of the month.

2. To have interviewed John about his absence record and agreed our next steps before the start of next month.

3. To have reduced average customer waiting time from ten minutes to eight minutes by the end of this season.

The objectives themselves should stem from your project plan and represent individuals' contributions to the project as a whole. The use of such objectives will not only help every member of staff see exactly how their job contributes to the achievement of the project as a whole, it will also help you to monitor progress and detect early warning signs that everything is not as it should be.

Getting the best from who you've got depends not only on motivation and objective setting, it also relies on the provision of appropriate development opportunities, both for individuals and for the team as a whole. If you are interested in these aspects of managing people you may like to have a look at another book in this Gower series, *Managing People*, which covers recruitment,

 Star Tip

The way leaders handle 'people' issues is one factor which distinguishes successful from less successful managers. But successful project management is not simply about 'management' as such – it is also about providing an appropriate level and style of leadership to your team.

selection and discipline as well as the performance issues outlined here.

STEP 2: INFLUENCE THOSE WHO ARE OUTSIDE THE TEAM

Because we all have to influence people who are outside our direct line of control it is very important to develop the skills to be able to handle this.

Hierarchy	**Charisma**	**Negotiation**
Where you rely on your status to get what you need (or want).	Where you achieve what you need through sheer force of personality.	Where you identify benefits that the other person wants and provide (some or all of) these in return for getting (some or all of) what you want.

There are several influencing techniques available to us, although some people will rely more heavily on some than others.

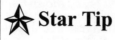
Star Tip

'Change is always a threat when it's done to me or imposed on me – whether I like it or not. But it is an opportunity if it's done by me. It's my chance to contribute and be recognized. That is the simple key to all of this: make it an opportunity for people and reward them for it.' Rosabeth Moss Kanter in *The Change Masters*.

Activity

What questions might you need to ask to identify an effective influencing strategy?

Who ...

How ...

What ...

How much ...

What more ...

Whichever you use, you will need to work out how best to apply it in order to maximize your chances of success.

As well as the obvious question: 'Who are the key influencers around here?' you might need to ask things such as:

❖ How could my project/my ideas help them achieve their objectives?
❖ What are the political implications of success and failure and hence, what are their actions likely to be?
❖ In particular, how much support are they likely to give my proposals?
❖ What more should I tell them about what I have to offer?

SKILLBUILDER

When determining your approach to a colleague it can be helpful to ask yourself the question: 'How would I want my colleague to behave if she were to be approaching me on this issue?'

You can then bear in mind the answers to these questions when thinking through how to specify the contribution your project can make to meeting the organization's goals.

 Vignette

My own preferred way of interacting is in terms of:

- ❖ Being honest but diplomatic
- ❖ Dealing with any concerns as soon as possible rather than allowing them to 'fester'
- ❖ Doing what I promise
- ❖ Treating people with respect – acknowledging everyone's right to an opinion and even their right to make mistakes

Unfortunately, this 'star tip' won't always work because everyone is different and will respond to things in different ways. Nevertheless, it does provide a framework for action.

You may also have thought of such things as:

- ❖ Finding out his or her preferred working style and adapting to it
- ❖ Some people like detail, others the big picture
  - • some like more reassurance than others that everything is under control

SKILLBUILDER

 **Activity**

Jo is a project manager who needs to persuade Hilary, a manager, to deliver a written set of requirements which Jo will rely on to steer the project. Delays to delivery will cause delays to the project start and to the eventual benefits. Jo is being measured by project overrun time and successful project completion.

Hilary is a manager who is under pressure to service customer requests. Hilary would like a new system to help with this work but has no time to set out the detailed requirements. Hilary is being measured against the number of satisfied customer requests within certain timescales and on numbers of complaints received.

❖ What questions should Jo be asking of Hilary?
❖ What points could Jo raise?
❖ What influencing techniques could Jo try?

• some want things in writing, others prefer to listen
❖ Always checking your facts, such as clarifying where your respective responsibilities start and end.

Jo needs to concentrate on the things that are important to Hilary – such as the number of satisfied customer requests and numbers of complaints – and explain to Hilary that the project will help to improve these and that the requirements are vital to delivering the benefits Hilary wants. There is no point in concentrating on Jo's targets as Hilary will not be motivated by these and they will be met anyway if Jo meets Hilary's expectations. So, Jo needs to be asking questions designed to find out what Hilary's interests are

UNIT 8 | Manage Quality

In this Unit, we will be covering the three actions you need to take to ensure quality in your project.

- **Set quality standards.**
- **Put in place procedures that are designed to meet those standards.**
- **Check that the outputs meet the standards**

Understanding these three actions will help you:

- reduce wasted effort on rework
- ensure acceptance of project deliverables.

Manage quality

STEP 1: DEFINE WHAT YOU MEAN BY QUALITY

We have already seen that quality – or functionality – is the third major element which needs to be incorporated into the structure of your project. You therefore need to take quality seriously.

We can think of quality as 'doing what is required' or as a relative measure of worth. Both are valid. How does this fit with the culture or expectations of your organization?

Sometimes you will need to follow organizational guidelines on quality. For example, if your organization has a quality policy that will also apply to your project this may already set out the criteria to be used for different product types.

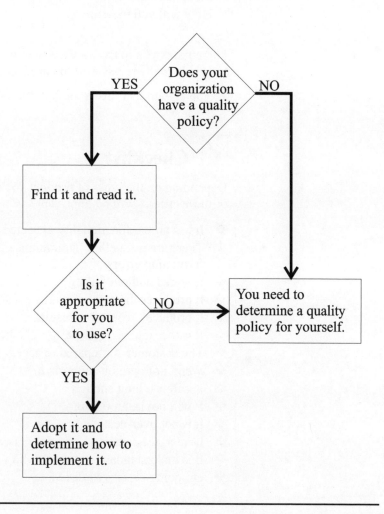

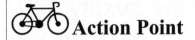 **Action Point**

Answer these questions:

❖ Who defines quality?
❖ What does 'quality' mean to your project – 'doing what is required' or 'a relative measure of worth'? – or something else?

STEP 2: SET YOUR QUALITY CRITERIA

However you answered the previous questions, you will need to be able to answer the following questions also:

❖ How will you know if what you produce is going to be acceptable?
❖ How will you measure it?

This requires you to have a very clear understanding of what is acceptable to the receiver of the product.

Are you certain that this is, in fact, the case?

 Checklist

Depending on the types of product you are to produce, which of these criteria will be important?

❖ It has all the functionality expected
❖ There are no spelling, grammatical, lexicographical or formatting errors
❖ It works without failing
❖ It produces the correct results consistently
❖ It produces acceptable results
❖ It is the right size, shape, weight etc.
❖ The customer is prepared to accept it
❖ Weight of opinion supports it
❖ It will last long enough
❖ It will not last too long
❖ It is not over-designed
❖ It interfaces with any other necessary products or systems
❖ It is understandable by those who will use it
❖ On-going costs are affordable

STEP 3: CARRY OUT CHECKING PROCESSES

You will also need to decide how you will check the quality of each product, when and by whom. You may need to plan in some elapsed time in order to ensure that these quality checks do not delay the rest of the project.

When you need to have something checked, you will need to supply that item, plus the product description (to check against) and any information about how the check should be performed. You might find it beneficial to write a short memo that can be photocopied or printed as a standard form and attached for the checkers, to explain the process. Leave a space where you can write in the date the check should be returned by, and where to return it.

To: reviewer

Subject: Quality Check

You have been provided with a copy of the product, its product description (which includes the quality criteria) and a response form. Please return all by 23 August.

I would like you to concentrate on criteria 1, 2, 5 and 6.

 Checklist

Ways of Checking

- ❖ Measure and compare to specification
- ❖ Try it out and see if it works
- ❖ 'Walk it through' – follow the process on paper without doing it for real
- ❖ 'Envelope' test it – use test conditions that check each of the extremes – highest, lowest, minimum, maximum, fastest, slowest and so forth
- ❖ Offer your opinion – about ease of use, factual correctness, suitability and such like
- ❖ Test it to destruction
- ❖ Test a sample – make sure that it is statistically significant
- ❖ Compare its result with those from the existing system or process

---

YOU MAY NOW CONTINUE WITH THE NEXT UNIT ON PAGE 139
OR MOVE TO THE SKILLBUILDER SECTION THAT FOLLOWS

Manage quality

STEP 1: DEFINE WHAT YOU MEAN BY QUALITY

You can incorporate quality into the structure of your projects by:

1

Ensuring that all involved – from Project Board down – have their responsibilities laid out at the start.

2

Introducing some formal quality methods.

Products

An emphasis on products, with Product Descriptions that include quality criteria and a definition of the quality check method to use, plus processes that will build in quality from the start, and quality checks to confirm this.

Project

Procedures for project level quality, such as how requests for changes and off-specifications can be dealt with and how risks will be managed.

Quality is thus not just a matter of checking a finished product to see if it is 'OK' but is, rather, a total process. That process starts with defining the product and what quality means for that product. It then means defining a system to develop the product right first time – and finally checking it against its criteria. All changes are looked at to see what effects they might have on products under way, products not yet started and products that have been finished and accepted but now need to be changed.

Consider this table showing how the two different definitions of quality as a minimum standard or as a relative measure of value might be viewed by two people with different expectations.

	Quality as a minimum standard	Quality as a relative measure
Someone seeking to reduce costs	Does it do the job – and no more? Extra cost for extra features is a waste.	What will the costs be over its life? Should I spend more now on something that will last longer or break down less frequently?
Someone seeking 'the best'	I have set my standards and I expect this to meet them. It's either right or it's not!	I will pay more if I can see an extra benefit.

If you are dealing with cost reducers, your project's own standards must match that philosophy – and the same goes for excellence-seekers.

STEP 2: SET YOUR QUALITY CRITERIA

Quality criteria can be objective or subjective that is, measurable facts or someone's opinion. However, even objective criteria often come from a subjective analysis of requirements.

For example, I might specify that the new desk your project is providing for me (as part of an office refurbishment project) should be at least 80cm deep by 160cm wide. When you deliver it to me, we can both check the dimensions. If the desk is 85cm by 165cm it clearly meets the criteria

- whoever measures it and no matter how often. However, the desk might still be too small for my needs. I just didn't realize that when I gave you the dimensions. The precise nature of the measurements hid the fact that I simply made them up!

It is therefore your job, as project manager, to ensure that the quality criteria are good ones – that they reflect the real needs for the products, regardless of what others might have told you.

 Checklist

Quality criteria can come from:

❖ The end user
❖ Management objectives
❖ Organizational standards
❖ National standards
❖ Requirements to fit in with other products, systems or outcomes
❖ Legislation or regulations
❖ Known best practice

 Fact File

To be able to offer NVQs, assessment centres need to be able to meet a number of criteria set down by the Qualifications and Curriculum Authority. These criteria are laid down in the form of a number of general requirements to do with centre management, systems and procedures to ensure quality and equality of opportunity and so on. Before becoming accredited, centres receive a visit from an 'external verifier' employed by the awarding body. This verifier examines evidence relating to each of the criteria and talks to the staff concerned. Any problems are discussed with the centre and an action plan agreed. Once approval to offer NVQs has been granted the verifier visits the centre at least twice a year to review the plan and ensure continued compliance with requirements.

In the case of an office move project with a floor diagram product, there may be specific quality criteria to specify the minimum distance between desks as well as criteria to conform to the requirements of the Workplace (Health, Safety and Welfare) Regulations 1992 Approved Code of Practice regarding the amount of space allocated per person.

You will have included details of any standards (project, organizational, national or international) that products have to conform to in your product descriptions. You will also have included more specific criteria for the product. How will you check that it satisfies its requirements?

Here is some guidance on what makes good quality criteria.

 **Guideline**

Quality criteria should be measurable. This might mean the objective sort of test we mentioned above or a subjective approval. If subjective, you should know whose judgement will be used and the basis on which they will use it.

Guideline

Criteria should be complete. They should cover every aspect of the product. You don't want to produce something that fails to gain acceptance because it doesn't do something that you didn't know it needed to.

Guideline

There should be an 'audit trail' from any discussions, proposals, business case, standards, legislation or whatever, to the criteria. So, you should be able to track back from each criterion to find out where it came from and hence its purpose and validity. Then, if the base situation changes, you will be able to renegotiate the quality criteria.

 **Guideline**

Identify who should check the product against each criterion. Not everyone need check all criteria. For example, some reviewers might need to check a report for factual accuracy, others for viability of recommendations and another person (possibly a specialist) for grammatical and other such errors.

STEP 3: CARRY OUT CHECKING PROCESSES

You can use either objective or subjective tests to undertake quality checks.

Objective

Objective tests are unarguable: either the product meets the criteria or it does not. The outcome of an objective test never varies, regardless of whoever undertakes the check, or how ever many times it is done. You can usefully apply objective tests to some physical products. For example, 'Is the height of a wall within the dimensional tolerance specified?' or 'Is a metal forging as hard as its specification dictates?' This type of test is also applicable to many software applications – again, either the program calculates correctly or it doesn't.

Subjective

Subjective tests, on the other hand, are a matter of opinion: one reviewer will be satisfied with the product and another will not. Nevertheless, many useful criteria come into this category, such as ease of use, validity of recommendations, comfort and even grammatical correctness. (Acceptable grammar changes over time and according to the type of document.)

 Activity

What sorts of check would you apply to these products?

❖ A final consultancy report
❖ A procedure for checking visitors through security
❖ An automated telephone response system

SKILLBUILDER

Final report

You could ask one person to check the spelling, grammar, format, page numbering and so forth. Participants could give opinions as to the accuracy of statements made. Another consultant could check the logical progression, from problem to solution. Potential users of the report could check the acceptability of recommendations.

Procedure

You could test it with a few 'guinea pigs' – members of staff playing the part of visitors. Then you could try it on a few real visitors, under close supervision.

Response system

You could try it out by calling in to the system and using each of the options in a logical manner, to test every one. If the system allows access to many extensions, you could try a sample from each department or each floor or location. You could measure performance in terms of response times. Then, you could ask some selected customers to give their opinions of it.

Subjective tests are normally more difficult to apply than objective ones. For instance, if we were to ask 12 readers whether or not this Workbook is sufficient for the needs of its defined market we may well get 12 rather different replies. Some people may consider that it covers all the ground in reasonable detail, but others may need much more detail in some areas. For others again, there might be too much detail in it. So whether it passes its quality check depends, to a degree, on who checks it. The same difficulty may apply to consultancy reports that have been commissioned as part of a project. People often have different views as to how a particular problem came about let alone how it should be solved!

PRINCE® defines a particular method of reviewing subjectively assessed products called a Formal Quality Review. This is useful for any item that needs subjective checking by a number of people.

Send a copy of the product (which is normally a document of some kind) to a number of reviewers. Where you cannot copy a product you may need to circulate it instead. Where appropriate, you may choose a different method: for example, if you need to have a model of a new building reviewed, you can let your reviewers know where they can view it, and when. They will need:

1	**2**	**3**
A copy of the Product Description against which to judge the product	A blank error list	Instructions and deadline

The reviewers put anything that they feel does not meet the Product Description onto the error list. Some sadistic people really enjoy working as reviewers, as it is not their job to suggest corrections, only to point out faults. Correction identification comes later and may itself be a matter of subjective judgement, to be decided alongside project timescales and other priorities.

Once they have completed their review, the reviewers return their error lists to the project administrator. The lists are then normally shown to the product's creator prior to a review meeting, so that the creator can prepare for the meeting. If you prefer, you can arrange for the errors to be collated and grouped but this is often more effort than it is worth.

 Activity

What would you expect to be the main purpose of a review meeting? Select just one from the following possibilities.

❖ To find out who is to blame for errors
❖ To come up with an agreed list of errors
❖ To plan how to put things right

The purpose of the review meeting is to agree a set of errors so the subjectivity of each reviewer is tempered by that of all the others. This means that if only one person considers something incorrect when the others consider it correct, it may not get added to the agreed list. Of course, errors picked up by one person may get missed by another so it is important not to go simply by the error lists. The product's creator may also be able to explain why something has been done and serve to answer questions about a particular potential error. You will see from this that 'error' is possibly too harsh a term at this stage, as the reviewers may well have picked up queries which the product creator is able to explain satisfactorily at that time.

After the review meeting, the agreed list of errors is passed to the person responsible for scheduling corrective work. That may be the creator, the team leader or the Project Manager. If the work requires substantial effort or endangers the timescales or costs of the project, this might also require that the Project Board be informed and even that a new plan be produced.

Guideline

You should also be clear that quality reviews are not the same as consultation. Some organizations send products for review as a way of gaining user approval, for example, when the users have never seen the product before. If you do this, expect long delays and many changes. It is ALWAYS better to consult first, incorporate the information gained (or explain why you can't) and build a product that is likely to satisfy all stakeholders and then ask them to review what they have been involved in to make sure that no errors have been made than to build in isolation in the forlorn hope that stakeholders will be satisfied with what you have produced. The consultation exercise results in a faster project, with fewer delays, fewer mistakes and a more committed and enthusiastic customer. I know of NO exceptions to this.

 **Guideline**

Finally, you will want to put your quality control and review procedures into context. Quality does not come free. All these processes have a cost. You will therefore want to be assured that the time and effort you put into managing quality has a payoff that is, that the costs of poor quality outweigh the costs of control.

 Real Life Story

It can be all too easy for reviewers to concentrate on the wrong level of error especially with documents.

I once worked on a £100 million project where the quality manager's chief concern was whether a document conformed to the organization's Quality Manual! Did the Project Initiation Document have all the right headings, suitably underlined in the right size? If not, the project would be delayed.

 Action Point

Take a look at just one of the processes undertaken in your project.

❖ What costs are involved in maintaining quality?
❖ How do the costs of conformance compare with those of non conformance?

UNIT 9   Manage Changes

In this Unit, we will be covering some ways of dealing with the inevitable pressures on you to change what is required of your project.

- **Deal with requests for change.**
- **Keep track of what you've produced.**

Understanding these aspects will help you:

- ensure that your project is not subject to unauthorized changes
- keep control of cost, quality and time
- ensure that you and your team are using a consistent set of products.

Manage changes

STEP 1: DEAL WITH REQUESTS FOR CHANGE

Projects are about change – but they are also subject to change themselves.

 Action Point

What sort of changes might be requested over the life of your project – and how might you deal with them?

Changes to scope	
Changes to assumptions	
Changes to constraints	
Changes to outcomes	
Changes to resources	

You need to assess the impact of the change:

✓ Check List

❖ What are the quality implications of the change – is it a real improvement? Does it matter? Will anyone notice?

❖ What are the likely costs of the change – in terms of money, manpower etc?

❖ What are the resource implications? Have you the right skills (or machinery) to do it?

❖ What are the timescale implications? Will the project overrun, and by how much? Will some milestones be late and what are the implications of that?

❖ What are the likely benefits? Reduced project costs, reduced running costs, improved functional ability?

❖ Who else would be affected by this change? Should you contact any of your stakeholders to find out their views?

How will you respond? Whatever the request and whatever your decision, you will want to follow a simple process:

Refer to Unit 6 for advice on solving problems and making decisions

 Check List

❖ Acknowledge the request formally (in writing or e-mail)

❖ Investigate the costs and benefits

❖ Decide on the action needed

❖ Tell the requester what has been decided

❖ Log the request, with all the investigation and decision-making information, for future reference

❖ If the work is to be done, schedule it into the plans

 Star Tip

Even if you decide to reject the request, keep the information. The same request could come up from a different source later, and it will save you time and effort if you do not have to go through it all again. Simply review the past information to see if it is still valid, update it and make a new decision.

STEP 2: KEEP TRACK OF WHAT YOU'VE PRODUCED

 Check List

❖ What products and resources do you deal with that you produce or come in different versions?

❖ How can you make sure you're using the correct version?

❖ How will you make sure that you can keep the product safe and secure against loss?

❖ How are you going to ensure that you are able to reproduce all valid configurations of what has been produced?

Not all of your project outcomes will have different versions –
and not all of those that do will warrant a system to handle them.
You only need to keep track of items that are likely to change
over the course of the project after they have been approved.

You can use a computer database for this – or a simple card
index. You might even consider a 'library ticket' system – where
project staff can book out a product they are working on.

Manage changes

STEP 1: DEAL WITH REQUESTS FOR CHANGE

You cannot avoid changes altogether – and even changes that can be avoided might be tackled better head on.

 Check List

The reasons for change are many and various, but might include the facts that:

❖ It is often not possible at the start of a project to know exactly what has to be done or what its sponsors want
❖ Requirements develop as the project progresses and these changes need to be accommodated
❖ Changes in the external environment also impact on a project. The need for whatever the project is producing may go away – or intensify – or just change
❖ Funds may become available that were not known about before – or become unavailable when they had been relied upon
❖ Project staff can change – by leaving, by taking unplanned time off sick, by becoming trained, by becoming experienced
❖ New external constraints may be applied – new laws or regulations, new organizational standards or edicts

Here are some likely changes. You may be able to think of others.

 Someone suggests a better way of doing something

 The estimates don't appear to be very accurate, so additional work is needed

 Someone wants something that was not in the original plan

 There are problems with getting approval for completed products, so additional work is needed

 A change is made to the scope, objectives or constraints of the project

 Someone leaves the project (or gets pulled off it)

 Someone joins the project (or gets assigned to it)

SKILLBUILDER

Real Life Story

One organization that I know of runs projects to develop complex systems over the course of a number of years. The end users of these systems have a say in defining them at the outset but they are then excluded from the design, development and construction phases in an attempt to ensure that the projects do not overrun. Not surprisingly, when the systems are eventually handed over the users often find that they no longer meet their requirements – the project has not incorporated the changes that should have occurred naturally over that period. To make matters worse, the restriction on change often does not even prevent the problems of late or over budget delivery that it was designed to!

However, I would not wish to suggest that tackling change is always straightforward. Sometimes, you will not know what led to the request and you then stand the danger of making a decision that turns out to have a larger impact than you expected. It is better to do some research before coming to a conclusion and, if necessary, referring upwards.

For example, suppose that Framlingtons is undertaking a project to build a road bridge over a river. For a while everything goes according to plan, but then the project manager receives a Request For Change suggesting that a new type of crash barrier be used at an additional cost. Despite the fact that the business case for the change might well be a good one, the project manager may find that he does not have the additional funds needed, or he may have the funds but be aware that there is a 'political' dimension to his decision the suggested barriers are British whereas the original ones are not. In these cases, a further outcome - referral to a higher authority - is the best option. For the project manager, that higher authority will be the Project Board or sponsor.

 Star Tip

If what you've done is wrong you need to do something about it. If it's an improvement you may or may not – it depends on your authority and your client.

You need to handle changes systematically, so that decisions can be taken about:

* which changes to adopt
* which to reject
* which to defer until later.

You will also need to decide:

* who else to involve
* whether the change is within your authorization limit
* whether it is likely to affect time, cost or quality.

In order to make those decisions, you need to obtain as much information as possible about the cost, time and quality implications of the change and the benefits ensuing as a result. You also need to keep records of what changes have been requested and what has happened to them, to ensure that:

* you can justify your actions later
* you can be sure that you have compared benefits and costs correctly
* project staff are working to the latest plan.

⤷ Guideline

A simple and effective method is to detail what the problem or suggestion is, either on a standard form or a free-form memo, depending on the organization's own procedures.

On receipt of the form it will be up to you, as the project manager (often by delegation to support staff) to decide what to do about it. You will need to decide whether to:

* accept the change request (in which case you need to schedule it in but not necessarily for immediate action)
* reject the change request
* refer the request to a higher level of authority (especially for a scope change, where you might be dealing with the closure of this project and the startup of another one)
* ask the requester if you can delay making the decision until a later time in the project when you will have additional information.

Costs of change

Changes will normally have an impact on costs – and history shows that this is normally upwards!

Often, the Request For Change will arise from the customers or sponsors and when this happens you need to make them fully aware of the costs of such a change. If the customers are willing to fund it, you must record this. You may also need to look at changing your contracts as a result of such changes. Every Request For Change that you adopt must be funded, and this must be recorded in the project files.

It is common practice in many industries (but by no means all) to allocate a contingency fund or a change control budget to deal with Requests For Change. It is important that this budget is used for the purpose it was intended and not for funding poor project control or poor quality work. You should find that the records arising from the changes will help you manage the change control budget.

STEP 2: KEEP TRACK OF WHAT YOU'VE PRODUCED

Depending on the nature of the project, you may find that you are producing more than one version of something – a report, a plan, a procedure, a design, a specification and so forth – or that you are working to specifications that change over time. You need to make sure that anyone who needs access to these has the latest version to work on, and that you hand over the correct version at the end of the project.

Jaresh needed to draft a contract for the purchase of some new equipment as part of a project. The contract wording depended upon pre-contract correspondence relating to the equipment specification, payment, terms and conditions. He drafted the contract and both his manager and the supplier signed it. Two months later, a dispute arose and his firm took the supplier to court - and lost. Jaresh had used an old specification while drafting the contract. The supplier had assumed they had simply changed their minds, so did not query it. The firm had to pay for the court costs, the supplier's legal bills and had to renegotiate the contract to bring it in line with the correct specification.

This problem could have been avoided by using proper version control. By recording versions of the specification, Jaresh would have known of the change immediately.

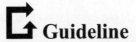

Guideline

Your version control system should record (as a minimum):

* ❖ The version number and date of each item produced
* ❖ Who is working on each item
* ❖ Who has a copy of each controlled item (or the original) so that they can be kept informed of changes.

Guideline

When someone needs access to a controlled item:

* ❖ They should ask for it and be given the latest version
* ❖ They should be told if someone else is working on that item and if someone else is working on something that relies on the item they are working on
* ❖ Anyone who is working on an item affected by this request should also be told.

The significance of this depends on the nature of your project. For example, if you are introducing computer equipment into an organization, you will need to know what updates to supply each person according to what versions of each hardware and software component they currently have. If an error occurs, you may be able to trace it back to a particular configuration using the techniques we introduced in Unit 6 (mysteries). That simplifies the problem-solving process.

You can use the records you keep of different configurations to help you determine the knock-on effects of changes. For example, if you find that you need to change one component in an assembly, what other components of that assembly will also need changing? Will any further changes be needed when that new assembly is itself incorporated into something?

Star Tip

Configuration records can be useful in operational management also, and you should consider making these part of the handover documentation at the end of the project. This will help to identify the same sorts of issues long after the project has finished.

Finally, it is well worth giving security and confidentiality procedures a thought every now and again. After all, if you are producing items that are to be stored outside, you will probably take measures to protect them. In an office, it is all too easy to ignore the protection that your project's outcomes deserve. You might therefore want to consider a 'product safe'. This is simply somewhere to store completed items so they do not get lost, damaged or stolen. This might be a physical safe for valuable items, or a fire safe, or just a lockable cabinet. For computer-produced items, it might be a backup tape or disk. Whatever form it takes, it ensures that you will never be in a position where the work you have done has been wasted through loss of the finished article.

 Real Life Story

Our own offices suffered a burst water pipe one Christmas. As we practise what we preach, all our computer data was backed up and held in a fireproof safe which was undamaged by the ensuing flood.

Summary of Part II

This Part has covered the actions you need to take during the running of your project. You may recall that we also said at the end of Part I that you should consider all of the preparation work as you proceed through the project, to check what has changed and decide what to do about it.

If there is one single message that needs to come out of all of this, it is that projects are about people – not technology, planning techniques, software schedulers, record-keeping or even finance. What makes the difference between a successful project and an unsuccessful one is likely to be how you dealt with the people involved – in your team, the stakeholders, customers, management or whoever.

Once you have established a good working practice to deal with people, you will find it so much easier to deal with the progress issues, change requests, problems and quality issues that we have covered in this Part.

Nevertheless, projects are prone to risks and to problems – so you should now take a few moments to look at the fault-finder that follows. Hopefully, it will give you some clues as to what to do if these situations occur.

Do not leave it until you approach the end of your project before reading Part III. You may find useful information there that you need to deal with in advance.

Progress Fault-finder

This fault-finder section covers the things that can go wrong while the project is in progress.

We have selected just a few of the common problems and suggested some causes and solutions. However, managing a project does not lend itself to 'colouring-by-numbers' and you may find that none of these problems trouble you – but that you have a completely different set. You may also find that the solutions we have given do not work in all cases. Nevertheless, we believe that they give a good starting point and may spark off some ideas about what is happening and how to deal with it.

If you want one piece of advice that will always help, the message is to communicate. People respond better when they are consulted – even if they do not support your project.

CHECKPOINT

Fault-finder

Problem or symptom	Likely cause(s)	Potential action(s)
Progress is slower than you expected.	A. People are not motivated or do not understand (or have) goals.	1. Use the advice in this Workbook to agree goals with your team. 2. Thank them for meeting deadlines and for good work. Show how their contribution has helped move the project along. 3. Explain to your team the importance of the project.
	B. Estimates are too optimistic or the job is more difficult than expected.	1. Use change control to re-plan the project. Incorporate all new information into your plan. 2. Find other resources to help – other people with more appropriate skills or tools that will speed up the process. 3. If the non-critical tasks are taking longer, you may need to take no action at this time.
	C. Lack of quality or lack of approval is creating more work.	1. Make sure that quality criteria are created for all outcomes and that people working on them are aware of the criteria and how they will be checked. 2. Get customers involved in creating the quality criteria. 3. Stress the importance of approval to the success of the project. Make sure it is not withheld unnecessarily.
	D. Project staff are introducing unauthorized changes.	1. Make sure that staff understand what they are supposed to be producing – use Product Descriptions. 2. Make sure that staff understand and use the change control procedures. 3. Persistently reject any product where unauthorized changes have been made.

CHECKPOINT

Fault-finder

Problem or symptom	Likely cause(s)	Potential action(s)
Things keep changing.	A. Genuine changes are occurring in the business.	1. You can do nothing to prevent changes to the business environment, but you may be able to foresee some of them. Update your risk plan to deal with them.
		2. Shorten your management control periods and review the purpose of the project and its continuing viability more frequently.
		3. Make sure that your change control procedures are watertight.
	B. Management or customers do not appreciate the effects of changes and are therefore introducing them without sufficient thought.	1. Explain what the changes are doing to the project by showing what additional expense and delay they cause.
		2. If the changes are small and frequent, show the cumulative effect and explain that it is not simply a single change that is causing the problem.
		3. Suggest that the change control procedure be used – and feed back costs and delays to management for approval.
	C. Internal politics.	1. Determine whether the changing circumstances are real or just power-plays by one faction to outwit another. Have nothing to do with artificial changes and publish memos and reports to senior management that highlight what is happening.
		2. Speak to the people concerned and explain that they must either agree on the outcomes or stop the project.

CHECKPOINT

Fault-finder

Problem or symptom	Likely cause(s)	Potential action(s)
It takes too long to get users and others outside the project to contribute – especially when checking products for quality or gaining approval.	A. Their priorities are not the same as yours.	1. Find out what their priorities are. You may find that you can convince them to increase the project's importance or you may find that the project has a greater influence on them than previously known.
		2. Apply power from your own management.
		3. Live with it and change your project plans – perhaps by rescheduling just their parts of the project to give them more time.
		4. Find someone else who is able to do the work instead.
	B. Internal politics.	1. Their delays may not be caused by overwork or lack of priority but by a reluctance to show approval – or even outright hostility to the project. You will need to determine what other pressure to apply to them – through higher levels of management, for example, or by playing tit-for-tat.
		2. Take another look at your stakeholder list. Can anyone else help you with this situation?
		3. You may need to revisit your risk plan to deal with this.

Fault-finder

Problem or symptom	Likely cause(s)	Potential action(s)
Your customer(s) and manager(s) seem to want different things from each other.	A. The project outcomes were not properly addressed at the start of the project.	1. Call a meeting urgently between all parties and sort out the outcomes now. Better late than never. 2. Use your change control procedures to record the changes and rework the project plan. 3. You may find that your project cannot address all matters and that a follow-on or parallel project is needed.
	B. Requirements have changed.	1. Call a meeting urgently between all parties and sort out the outcomes now. Better late than never. 2. Use your change control procedures to record the changes and rework the project plan. 3. You may find that your project cannot address all matters and that a follow-on or parallel project is needed.

'Is this goodbye – or just au revoir?'

What to do to finish your project and how to evaluate its success

By the end of this Part you will be able to:

- recognize when to close your project
- decide what actions are needed to close it
- learn lessons about your project to assist you in the future
- prepare for the evaluation of the project's benefits.

If you are confident that you can already answer 'Yes' to most or all of the following questions you might like simply to refresh your memory by scanning the Fast Track pages in each Unit.

When you have completed this Part, review the Checkpoints at the end of all three Parts.

Self assessment checklist: Part 1	
I am confident that I can:	Yes ☑ No ☒
Recognize when to continue with a project and when to stop it prematurely.	
Recognize when to close a project as planned and when to extend it.	
Manage the handover of project deliverables to the end user or customer.	
Perform all the procedural actions necessary to cease work on the project.	
Identify lessons that will help me plan and manage future projects more effectively.	
Identify follow-on projects.	
Put in place the necessary records and procedures for eventual evaluation of benefits.	

Close the Project

In this Unit, we will be covering how to handle the two situations in which a project finishes.

- **Completing the project.**
- **Stopping an incomplete project.**

Understanding these two situations will help you:

- ensure that all necessary actions have been taken before project resources are released
- put in place any follow-on actions for review and evaluation.

Close the project

STEP 1: DECIDE WHEN TO END THE PROJECT

How will you know when to stop the project?

While this seems a fairly simple question, there is more than one answer to it:

- ❖ When the project plan has been completed
- ❖ When all the deliverables have been handed over
- ❖ When you need to stop it early, for any reason

Vignette

Many projects follow what has become know as the Magnus Magnusson syndrome – 'I've started so I'll finish' –

regardless of their ability to deliver further benefits or the need for the project at all.

In any project, the costs and benefits will follow a pattern set out during planning. Often, the marginal benefits achieved at the end of a project are not worth the marginal costs of achieving them. When costs exceed benefits, it is time to stop the project.

If the project's purpose disappears it is also time to call a halt. For example,

Christine's project had been set up to install a gymnasium in the building for the use of all staff, as part of their package of benefits. This high-tech studio was to be fitted out with new sprung flooring, mirrored walls and a sound system, before equipping it with

steppers, jogging machines, 'pec' decks and the like. The adjacent showers were to be state-of-the-art. No one told Christine about the firm's decision to move to new premises in six months' time, so she carried on spending the money on refurbishment right up to the day they packed their bags and left.

In this case, the project should have been put on hold when the likelihood of moving became known, and stopped immediately when the decision had been taken to move. (If the decision had been made to stay where they were, the project could then have been restarted.) A follow-on project could have been commenced to install a gym in the new building perhaps before the move of staff took place.

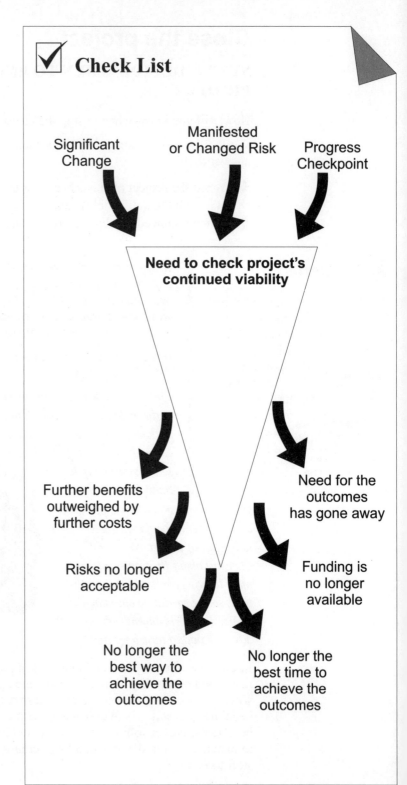

Action Point

Consider how you can keep track of the project's continued viability and need. Can any of the stakeholders help you with this information?

STEP 2: MANAGE THE CLOSEDOWN

Closing the project requires you to do many things:

- ❖ Hand over all products or outcomes
- ❖ Get acceptance of these
- ❖ Complete the documentation
- ❖ Dispense with project staff
- ❖ Update internal procedures – for example, so that no one can book time to the project any more
- ❖ File everything away
- ❖ Make a clear move to your next job

Check List

When planning for handover, you should also consider the following factors:

- ❖ Who will own the intellectual property rights – designs, for instance? Do you retain these or pass them to the customer?
- ❖ Who will be responsible for future design and development?
- ❖ Who will be responsible for operation or production?
- ❖ Who will be responsible for servicing and maintenance?
- ❖ How will payment be made?
- ❖ How will you ensure that all personnel and goods not to be transferred will be removed before transfer – especially if there is a continuous process involved which cannot be interrupted?
- ❖ Does what you are handing over comply with all statutory regulations – especially Health and Safety, Environmental, Employment?
- ❖ Is a commissioning period required, during which you will continue to provide services to the customer, although ownership may already have passed?
- ❖ If operation of the products is regulated, has the regulator been involved in their approval, and has approval been granted?
- ❖ What method of transfer will be used? For example, is a formal letter of acceptance enough, or must a legal transfer (such as a Deed) be prepared? Will there be a 'ceremony of the keys'?

You may have organizational procedures to cater for at least some of the requirements. Do you? How can you find out?

YOU MAY NOW CONTINUE WITH THE NEXT UNIT ON PAGE 179
OR MOVE TO THE SKILLBUILDER SECTION THAT FOLLOWS

Close the project

STEP 1: DECIDE WHEN TO END THE PROJECT

The British Standard Guide to Project Management (BS6079: 1996) gives an example of a project with project closure as the time when the whole system, building, work or whatever finally comes to an end. An example of this would be the decommissioning of a power station after 30 years of operation. Most project managers' definition of a 'project' is slightly different. They would normally say that a project comes to an end when the deliverables are delivered. This might be when a computer program has been written and passed into use, when a building has been built and is ready for occupation, or when the car has been designed and manufacturing begun.

 **Action Point**

Find out which definition your own organization uses. This may not be written down anywhere, but you might be able to determine it by looking at past or present projects. If you are currently running a project – or planning one – this may also be described in the project's scope.

 **Star Tip**

In the overall euphoria of ending the project – and the desire to do anything to achieve it – project managers can fall prey to the wily customer who, using a well-known negotiation trick, ask for 'just one little change' before they accept the project. These 'little changes' add up and you have no budget or time for them. Resist them and suggest they are tackled either during maintenance or in a follow-on project.

If you take the first definition of a project the British Standard one then project closure is the end of the matter; there is nothing beyond it except, perhaps, for a follow-on project to provide a replacement.

Under the more conventional definition, however, there is usually something to follow on from your project – normal operations. It therefore follows that you will need to cater for that when you complete your project. The project closure procedure has to make sure that your deliverables are properly implemented and passed to the users and that any faults with them are corrected before you finally relinquish responsibility. Either way, you would be advised to check that your sponsor or Project Board is in agreement that the project is complete; you may have some organizational procedures for this but if you do not you might like to design some.

Even so, it is sometimes not too clear where a project is expected to close. In IT projects where a program might be written, data converted and the whole system mounted onto new hardware and passed to the users, it is almost impossible to produce an error-free computer program first time. Invariably, some sort of error will exist within the system and whose responsibility is it to correct that? If the project closes when the system is delivered, then any faults will have to be sorted out by the users, possibly as part of a maintenance programme.

Rather than closing the project on delivery, it might be better, under those circumstances, to keep the project going for a while perhaps a month, two months or three months depending on how critical it is to allow for a 'bedding-in' period while the software gets debugged. You can use the same period for ensuring that the users are properly trained and that the documentation is understandable, and also to ensure that any backup or archiving procedures are being properly managed. If you do this, you can then close your project when the system is stable.

If project success is measured on the basis of the quality of its products this must be a better way of managing closure than simply handing over something that doesn't work. Having said that, there may still be small errors in the system that have to be handled by maintenance. In this case it becomes a matter of judgement as to where the cut-off point is. Either way, however, you may still need to undertake some further work relating to the value of the project procedures overall.

Fact File

There is a relationship between the lifecycle of the product and the lifecycle of the project. The two overlap for the stages shown in the diagram and have separate lives at other times.

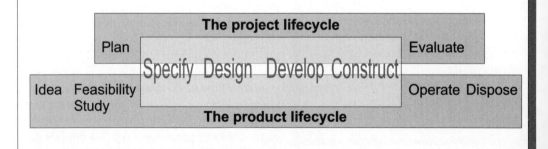

Additionally, you may well need to check that your outputs are delivering the benefits as predicted by the business case a little while after you have completed your project. This is something we take up in the final Unit.

Finally, your project might not be complete but you still need to close it. This can happen for a variety of reasons, including:

❖ Unmitigated disaster – the project is not producing the required outcomes and it seems likely it never will

❖ The costs of the project are forecast to rise to more than the benefits are worth

❖ The reason for the project has gone away

❖ A better way of achieving the required outcomes has been discovered

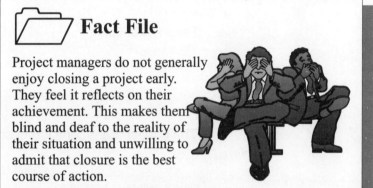

Fact File

Project managers do not generally enjoy closing a project early. They feel it reflects on their achievement. This makes them blind and deaf to the reality of their situation and unwilling to admit that closure is the best course of action.

However, some of the reasons we listed are outside the influence of the project manager and closing the project in these circumstances reflects well on a project manager who has monitored the situation closely enough to be able to tell, and who has the courage to take the right decision.

STEP 2: MANAGE THE CLOSEDOWN

You need to manage the closedown of the project to make sure that all necessary paperwork is complete, that resources are reassigned and that ownership of the outcomes of the project is properly established.

Some project managers find that, after the project has been completed, they remain the person to whom all enquiries are made even though they have moved on to another project. Part of the handover process has to ensure that any outcomes are self-sustaining, which could mean that the project must set up a maintenance system or train someone in how to support the outcomes after the project has closed.

 **Activity**

If you are coming to the end of your project, consider how this continuing support will be provided. You may need to request a change to the project to deal with this. This will contribute to the continued success of the project's work and ensure that you make a clean break from it, so you can concentrate on future work.

Where might you find the answers? Circle all of the following that you think might apply.

The initial contract — The post project review

Monitoring information **Product descriptions**

Changes agreed during the project

The project manager's job description

Product breakdown structure

Quality assurance system

Work breakdown structure

Most of these should have formed part of the initial contract, which you should now check. Also check any agreed changes during the project, to ensure that you have a complete picture of the current situation.

You can also use your Work Breakdown Structure or Product Breakdown Structure to help you to monitor progress towards the handover. These will enable you to check that all necessary work has been performed and all necessary products produced, in readiness for handover. Where Product Descriptions have been accepted by the customer or, better still, prepared by the customer, these will form part of the contractual documentation for acceptance of the project's outputs.

The Quality Assurance system will also provide information with regard to the acceptance of products – so preventing a customer from rejecting something they had previously accepted. Indeed, the handover process itself should be governed by the QA system just as much as any other part of the project, with quality documentation produced.

This guidance can be used not just at the completion of a project, but also where items are delivered incrementally during the project. You can monitor progress toward project handover at the end of each stage, so that a complete ownership and operation picture is produced.

From the possible answers above, then, only the post project review (because you won't yet have it available) and the project manager's job description (because it is unlikely to contain such information) are not relevant here.

 Star Tip

As we have seen throughout this Workbook, it is good practice to document the project. This will help others to plan and manage future projects and may also help in establishing maintenance programmes perhaps by reference to information such as the configuration management records we referred to in Unit 9. There are legal requirements for retaining accounting and some other information and you will need to deal with this also.

 **Action Point**

Find out all the legal requirements relating to your project's paperwork. How can you ensure that you comply?

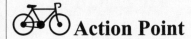 **Action Point**

You should also gather together all the accepted change requests, as mentioned in Unit 9, to pass on to whoever will be evaluating the project. They need this information to enable them to compare results with the original baseline and any changes to it. Make sure that files are up-to-date and properly filed away. They will be needed during the project evaluation process.

We take up the issue of learning lessons and documenting these in the final Unit.

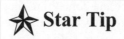

★ Star Tip

Place a label on each of your record folders and binders to shown when it can be disposed of. This will save time later – perhaps in many years' time. Accounting records need to be kept for at least six years.

Reassigning resources

The end of a project also leads to the need to redeploy the project staff. As project manager you will need to choose from a number of alternative options, many of which are heavily circumscribed by the law.

Which of the following alternative actions would you want to consider? Tick all those which apply.

❖ Doing nothing
❖ Retraining for alternative work
❖ Redeployment to another project or site
❖ Implementing your redundancy policy
❖ What other options might you have?

In fact, any of these options would be worth considering, depending on the particular situation you are in. Let's look at what I mean by this.

Do nothing

Contrary to what you might be thinking, this is not necessarily a 'cop out'. In fact, it is the first option to consider, although even doing nothing can still involve you in a certain amount of work.

It is likely to prove a particularly attractive option in the following situations:

❖ When there is an ongoing need either within or outside the project such as systems maintenance or actually running the operation that the project was set up for and your staff have the skills and inclination to continue.
❖ When staff had been engaged on fixed term contracts, which are now coming to an end. In this case you may want to check that they have received confirmation of their situation and understand what they need to do when they leave.

Retrain

The feasibility of this option will depend on a number of factors, such as:

❖ The need for staff elsewhere in the organization
❖ The aptitude of the staff to be retrained
❖ Their willingness to be retrained
❖ The time and cost involved versus the likely benefits (such as the ability to retain staff who know the organization and who are known by it, or the likelihood of being able to attract suitable new recruits relatively easily from outside)
❖ The relative level of the new work compared to the old. If it is of significantly lower status you could find that people refuse the work and claim redundancy instead, even if you agree to 'red circle' it – that is, to continue to pay at the old rate.

Although it can be seen as an expensive option, retraining may well have unexpected payoffs in terms of staff morale and commitment to an organization which is prepared to invest so heavily to prevent having to lay people off.

Redeploy

Again, this may or may not be a feasible option, although it is something you will want to plan for where possible if you are managing a programme. Even if you have another project or site with a staffing need you will have to look at the contractual position of those you are hoping to move on. If they have a locational flexibility clause in their contracts, and if you provide sufficient notice and take people's personal circumstances into account, you should be able to insist on redeployment.

Redundancy

Redeployment can also provide payoffs in terms of your liability for redundancy pay. If staff unreasonably refuse alternative work which offers the same sort of status and benefits as their previous work you are entitled to dismiss them without payment of redundancy pay (although of course they would still enjoy the normal legal protection from a dismissal which is unfair). If the work is very different they have the right to try it out for a few weeks. If, at the end of that period, either they or you decide that the work is not suitable you can make them redundant although, in this case, they would retain their right to redundancy payments.

Transfer

Special legislation applies in the situation where one organization takes on the responsibility for doing something previously done by another organization, to ensure that redundancy and employment rights are not avoided by a simple transfer of contract. The Collective Redundancy and Transfer of Undertakings (Protection of Employment) Regulations 1981 (and as subsequently amended) apply to any situation in which work done during the project will continue in some form after its end by another employer. In these circumstances, the staff working on the project may have the right to be transferred to the operating employer. The legislation, however, is complex, since it deals with the rights of individuals in a wide variety of transfer situations, and you should obtain professional legal advice if you think it might apply to you.

Here are some guidelines for you, if you need to redeploy people.

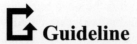

Guideline

Consult those involved. Even if there is very little room for manoeuvre you still need to discuss the situation with the staff involved so that they are fully aware of their options. They may have some useful suggestions for the way the redeployment is implemented or even some ideas concerning their current project which may make the redeployment unnecessary.

Guideline

Make proper handover and induction arrangements. Unless the need for your people's current work has ceased altogether it is likely that there will be some work that remains to be done over the course of the following few weeks or months. You will need to discuss how best to handle this with all those affected.

Just as importantly, you will want to ensure that the receiving department is prepared for the new arrivals and undertakes an adequate induction with them.

Guideline

Involve Trade Union officials if you recognize a trade union for bargaining or consultation purposes. You will need to bear in mind the type of information that trade union officials have a right to receive. This will normally be restricted to the type and number of people involved, but not necessarily to the names of individuals particularly those who are not Union members.

Ownership of outcomes

It is imperative that the outcomes of the project are delivered to their rightful recipient, and that they are accepted. If you do not gain acceptance, your project will rumble on. This is a matter of gaining agreement of what is expected and how it will be checked as being acceptable issues we covered in Unit 8.

Equally important is the need to ensure that the outcome owner is able to handle the work associated with maintaining the outcomes. For example, if you have delivered a new business process to the process owner, that person needs to be able to update it, document the changes, gain approval and so forth. You will be doing other work and you do not want to be interrupted by someone who still considers you to be the person responsible for the business process's upkeep.

While this may not seem a huge problem, it can turn into one quite quickly as you go from project to project. You can end up with a shopping basket of responsibilities, some dating from years back. You will probably not be able to book your time to them when you do them, so the effect of all this maintenance work will be seen simply through the less effective management of your current projects.

You will therefore need to ensure, during the project, that such issues are addressed. This might require some documentation to pass over, or some additional piece of equipment. It might require that you arrange training for the outcome owner, which itself could be a standard course or might need to be developed as part of the project.

Real Life Story

Trexopal

While delivering a project management training course to Trexopal (not their real name) it transpired that one of the problems encountered by project managers was that, after their project was completed and the goods handed over to others in the same organization, staff would still approach them with any queries or requests for maintenance. It was as if they were forever associated with that item, which put them under increasing stress as their successes mounted up. We identified that they were not performing a proper handover on project completion. They were therefore given the task of identifying at the start of each project who would be responsible for taking on the work after the project closed. Part of the project was then to plan for handover to that person, including any training they require.

Evaluate Success

In this Unit, we will be covering ways of determining whether your project was as successful as it could have been.

- **Learning lessons about managing projects.**
- **Identifying follow-on projects.**
- **Measuring costs and benefits.**

Understanding these three areas will help you:

- manage your future projects better
- disseminate good project management practice through your organization
- improve your business cases in the future
- identify future projects.

Evaluate success

STEP 1: LEARN LESSONS

Projects rarely go precisely to plan. However, we can use the inevitable changes, problems and risks as opportunities to learn new ways of managing and to add to our body of knowledge about what works and what does not. In that way, we can improve our chances of success for future projects.

Look back over the project and make an honest judgement about how you performed in the following areas:

 Checklist

- ❖ Did you identify all the outcomes – final and intermediate – at the start of the project? What else could you have done, with hindsight, to identify ones that popped up later?
- ❖ How close were your estimates of time and cost? How could you improve on your estimating procedures? Can you record your actual performance now, for use in future estimating?
- ❖ How accurate were your assessments of the skills, knowledge and attitudes needed of the project staff? What can you do to improve on this in the future?
- ❖ Did you identify all the stakeholders? Were your analyses of them correct?
- ❖ Did you do the work in the best sequence? How would you do it now, given the information you have?
- ❖ Did you identify all the risks that occurred? Did you spend too much effort on 'ghost' risks – the ones that seemed real but were not?
- ❖ Did you monitor the right things to enable you to measure progress? What should you have monitored?
- ❖ What progressing action did you take and what do you now wish you had done to keep the project on track?
- ❖ When you found a problem, are you satisfied that you dealt with it effectively? How would you now deal with it?
- ❖ You cannot change the decisions you made, but if you were to go back and make them again, would you do the same things? If not, why not?
- ❖ Did you motivate your team? If not, what else could you have done?
- ❖ How effective were you at influencing those outside your team? What else could you have done?
- ❖ Were your quality procedures adequate? How would you change them?
- ❖ Did you stick to your quality procedures? If not, what effect did this have? What would make you stick to them in the future?
- ❖ How did you handle requests for change? Did you accept the right changes and reject the others? Did you manage changes formally, staying 'on the ball' or did it all seem to slip away from you? How could you manage them more effectively next time?
- ❖ Did you manage to close the project cleanly, or are you still stuck with bits of it? Now what are you going to do about that?

You will find suggestions for all of these in the relevant Skillbuilder sections in this Workbook. However, there is nothing as effective as your own experience in teaching you lessons. Make sure that you grab this opportunity to do just that.

STEP 2: IDENTIFY FOLLOW-ON PROJECTS

Projects are about introducing change, and the changes they introduce can lead to the need for further changes. Often, further needs will be identified as a project progresses. Some of these can be handled by changing the current project. Others are better dealt with by a follow-on project. For example,

Axymet was nearing completion of its Investors in People project. During the project, a number of issues had arisen to do with ongoing staff training, and pressures had been applied to include the development of a new learning resource centre as part of the project. It was decided that this would extend the project's scope too far and endanger its control and evaluation. A follow-on project was therefore planned for the learning resource centre work.

 **Action Point**

Identify further projects you now consider could be beneficial.

❖ Who would be responsible for further work on the feasibility of these?
❖ If you know them to be feasible, are you interested in managing them?
❖ Who will you approach to do this?
❖ What arguments will you apply to persuade them to let you?

Checklist

Here are some questions to help you identify follow-on projects.

❖ Could the outcomes of the project be improved, now that you and the outcome owners have a better understanding of them?
❖ Were there further projects planned initially?
❖ Is there anything else that the owners of this project's outcomes could now do with?
❖ Could anyone else benefit from a similar project?
❖ Are there any outstanding project issues that could lead to a further project?
❖ Did the work on the project produce any flashes of inspiration about future projects?
❖ Does the work of managing the project itself lead you to think of further projects such as the introduction of standard project management methods?

STEP 3: MEASURE BENEFITS AND COSTS

It can be very difficult to measure the effectiveness of the project in terms of its costs and benefits.

Costs are usually fairly well known, but how will you check that the benefits, as originally planned and taking into account any change requests that were agreed, have actually been gained?

How do you know that the benefits are the results of this project, and would not have occurred anyway?

The effectiveness of training has long been the subject of discussion. It can be difficult to measure – and therefore difficult to justify to those who want firm figures on which to base their approval. One model, described by Kirkpatrick in his 1994 book *Evaluating Training Programmes: The Four Levels*, identifies four levels of measurement. This model, suitably adapted, can be used to help measure the success of projects. We have come up with the following four levels of evaluation.

Did the project deliver the items it was supposed to? Did they cost what was expected?

2

Are people now using them? Are they working in the manner expected? If time savings or other performance improvements were cited, are these being achieved?

3

Do the performance improvements make a difference to the working practices and outputs of the department or organization concerned? Does anyone notice?

4

Is the company's profitability improved? For charities and other not-for-profit organizations, what difference has it made to your ability to perform your mission?

Evaluate success

STEP 1: LEARN LESSONS

It is customary at the end of a project to write some sort of report about how the project itself was managed. This would include such things as an analysis of how the project went asking such things as: 'What went wrong?' and 'What could we do better next time?' – the 'Lessons Learned' report. The idea behind this is that any future project will be able to benefit from any lessons learned from your project.

You will want to consult all those who have had any involvement in the project, to gather their views on its success and any improvements that could have been made.

 Activity

What would you see as the advantages and disadvantages of the 'lessons learned' approach?

I would see the advantages as …

The disadvantages would include …

SKILLBUILDER

Unfortunately, most organizations do not have a mechanism for storing such lessons or disseminating them to those who will be managing projects in the future. In addition, whilst project managers starting up a project are interested in gaining as much information as they can about estimating and costs and benefits – the sorts of things that might well be available from the reports of other projects – when it comes time to close a project the project manager normally has very little incentive to add that sort of data into any system. For a start, at the end of a project there is very little time and probably no spare resource while everything gets sorted out and packed away. Secondly, learning a lesson inevitably means that something wasn't quite right and project managers are not well renowned for baring their souls at the end of their project and admitting to what went wrong! So, whilst it is good in theory, in practice it happens too infrequently.

STEP 2: IDENTIFY FOLLOW-ON PROJECTS

When your project is complete or when it has been stopped early you need to consider what further projects could be beneficial. Projects rarely exist in isolation and are often simply a step in the development of an organization's progress from where it used to be to where it wants to get to.

As your project comes to an end or during the evaluation of it you should determine what ideas and issues have been raised. These might have come from project issues (as in Unit 9) that your project could not accommodate. They might be new ideas that have come about as a result of the success (or otherwise) of your project.

Sometimes, projects are initiated as part of a series. For example, you might have performed a project to introduce a new training programme for sales staff. It was intended that, if successful, this should be followed by a project to develop training for customer care staff. Having completed the first project, should the second go ahead? It is likely that the situation will have changed since the idea was first presented, and this

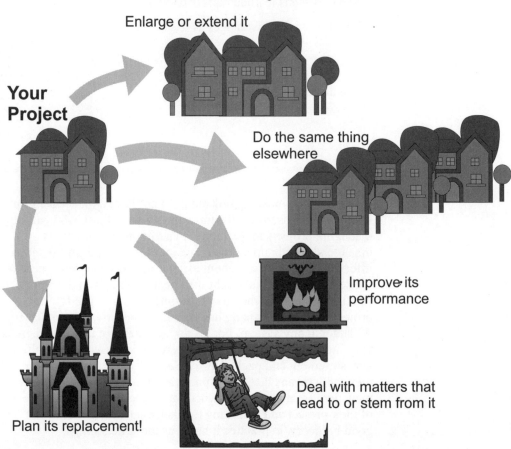

Enlarge or extend it

Your Project

Do the same thing elsewhere

Improve its performance

Deal with matters that lead to or stem from it

Plan its replacement!

now needs to be reevaluated.

STEP 3: MEASURE BENEFITS AND COSTS

The post project review is the process of analysing the value of the project. It is during the post project review that a reviewer will decide whether the expected benefits are being delivered. This can be carried out as a one-off exercise or as an ongoing programme, depending on the nature of the project's deliverables.

So, if the project delivers a new system (manual or automated) you might decide to wait for some time after the end of the project to allow for a bedding-in period and to allow people to get used to the system. It is also possible that the use of the system and the benefits that it delivers will change over time. If a system has been delivered for use over a number of years, it might be appropriate to undertake a number of reviews perhaps every six months or so to ensure that the benefits continue to flow as predicted. By highlighting any discrepancies between expected and actual benefits gained these post project reviews can also lead to maintenance work or the production of a project brief for one or more follow-on projects.

Even where you may think that the project's deliverables are immediately measurable – the construction of a new house, for example – it is likely that some time will be needed before a complete evaluation will be possible.

Sparkel

Sparkel had just completed a nine-month project to update its shop front with bright new fittings and window dressings. They found that sales increased by 20 per cent and concluded that the project was a success.

Grabbit

Grabbit had not made any significant changes to its shop front for some time. Sales increased by around 20 per cent when the new car park was built in town and the department store opened nearby.

Consider the following two situations.

When evaluating their project, Sparkel could not know what level of sales they could have expected had they not gone ahead with it. Their conclusion that the benefits came from their project is an understandable one, but not necessarily true. This phenomenon is called 'additionality' – what benefit the project added over what would have happened anyway.

We introduced a model in Fast Track to help you evaluate your projects. It shows four stages of benefit and hence four levels at which benefits can be measured. We repeat the model here with

SKILLBUILDER

1

Did the project deliver the items it was supposed to? Did they cost what was expected?	Use your project monitoring and control information to help you answer these questions.

2

Are people now using them? Are they working in the manner expected? If time savings or other performance improvements were cited, are these being achieved?	You will need to get data from your users for your answers here.

3

Do the performance improvements make a difference to the working practices and outputs of the department or organization concerned? Does anyone notice?	Speak to managers for an initial impression. Can you access customer complaint logs, sales figures, downtime or such like?

4

Is the company's profitability improved? For charities and other not-for-profit organizations, what difference has it made to your ability to perform your mission?	Again, you will need to find out from your user department or organizational statistics.

some advice on how to go about measuring the different levels of benefit achieved.

You could use questionnaires, interviews, observation, discussion or possibly available organizational information which may indicate the changes that you could reasonably attribute to the project. However, be aware that other changes will have taken place in the same time that your project was running and you may not be able to separate out the effects of

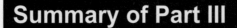

Summary of Part III

Now that you have finished Part III of the Workbook, you will be aware of the pitfalls that await the project manager who loses sight of the final goal – handover. In the excitement of planning a project, it is easy to concentrate on the techniques of planning, the negotiations over money or other resources and the identification of risks, without considering properly how the project will close.

You now know that it is vitally important that the handover criteria are understood at the start and built into the Product Descriptions. Unless this is done, you may end up with a project that can never end – and you can never move on in your project management career.

To gain the most from this Workbook, go back to the start and take another look at Part I. If you filled in the forms and completed the various exercises, would you give the same responses now? How different would they be? If you do this you will learn additional lessons – which is just what this Workbook has been designed for. We wish you well in your next project.

CHECKPOINT

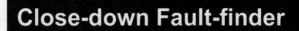

Close-down Fault-finder

This is the final fault-finder of the Workbook. It deals with both the handover period and the lessons learned.

As we have mentioned before about our checklists, tables and advice, feel free to add your own suggestions – and those you collect from colleagues – to the fault-finder.

Fault-finder

Problem or symptom	Likely cause(s)	Potential action(s)
Extra requirements keep being introduced that keep the project going.	A. The customer is finding out what was really wanted and gaining knowledge as outcomes are delivered.	1. While it would have been better to sort these out at the start, it is not always easy to specify one's requirements for something that has never been done before. You may therefore need to accept this situation – although it should be handled through the change request procedure.
		2. Small changes may be capable of addressing through some sort of maintenance programme that the customer can manage for himself.
		3. Larger changes may be better handled through a follow-on project, to ensure that costs and benefits are properly accounted for and the whole matter put into its correct position with regard to the organization's priorities.
	B. Outcomes were not agreed at the start of the project or the customer has not been sufficiently involved during their production.	1. Better late than never, attempt to gain some agreement on what would now be acceptable. This might not be the same as if agreement had been reached at the start and may simply be a negotiated settlement based on what is available now.
		2. Learn a lesson for next time!

Fault-finder

Problem or symptom	Likely cause(s)	Potential action(s)
The outcomes are continually rejected by the customer.	A. Quality criteria were not previously agreed with the customer.	1. Better late than never, agree them now – or as closely as you can. 2. Find out what *specifically* the customer is objecting to. Gain agreement on everything else and address the specific issues. Then gain agreement that you have tackled those. Do not readdress previously accepted criteria.
	B. The customer's requirements have changed.	1. Find out what the changes are. Use the change control procedure. 2. If necessary, you may need to deal with large changes in a follow-on project. 3. In any case, make sure that the customer knows what the costs of the changes will be – and get formal approval.
	C. The outcomes do not meet the criteria.	1. Your quality procedures have apparently not worked and you will need to accept responsibility for any corrective work. 2. You may be able to negotiate acceptance of some outcomes, thus reducing the size of the problem.
	D. The customer is not willing to take responsibility for the outcomes.	1. Like it or not they will have to do so sooner or later – so your job is to persuade, not to delay the inevitable. 2. Can you offer them training, hand-holding support, written instructions or anything else to make acceptance easier? 3. Can you show them that they can be confident in the outcomes? 4. Can you apply pressures from other stakeholders?

Fault-finder

Problem or symptom	Likely cause(s)	Potential action(s)
There is nowhere to lodge the lessons learned so that others can benefit from them.	A. These have not so far been seen as beneficial.	1. Stress how others could use them to shorten timescales, reduce costs and avoid or mitigate risks. 2. Consider what the effect would have been on your own project had you known when planning what you know now. Use those arguments to obtain a process for distributing lessons learned. 3. Keep your own log and share it informally with others.
	B. There is no one available to look after the report.	1. Can you identify the most logical owner of such lessons – a project or programme support office, for instance? 2. Why not look after it yourself? You could become the organization's 'projects guru'.
	C. It's a new idea and has not been set up yet.	1. As above, decide who should set this up and in what form. Should it be computerized or just a manual record? 2. When it has been set up, find out what other projects have recently completed and get their project managers to contribute. 3. Spread the word through current projects, so that the managers of these start to collect the lessons from them prior to their conclusion.

The whole subject of project management is vast and there are many other sources of information for you to use, depending on your own areas of interest. Here is our selection, together with details of books referred to in the Workbook.

Professional Body

The Association for Project Management
Thornton House, 150 West Wycombe Road,
High Wycombe, Bucks, HP12 3AE
Tel: 01494 440090. Fax: 01494 528937.
E-mail: secretariat@apm-uk.demon.co.uk

PRINCE method

Managing Successful Projects with PRINCE 2
1998. Norwich: The Stationery Office Ltd.

Further Avenues to Explore

Evaluating Training Programmes: The Four Levels
Kirkpatrick, D.L., 1994. San Francisco: McGraw Hill.

Team Roles at Work
Belbin, M., 1993. Oxford: Butterworth Heinemann.

Professional Qualification

Project Management (NVQ Levels 4 & 5)
Executive Plus Series Open Learning Pack
Churchouse, C. & J., 1998. Warminster: Mind*Shift* Ltd.

CHECKPOINT